TURNING

THE MIND

INTO AN

ALLY

RIVERHEAD BOOKS

a member of Penguin Putnam Inc.

2003

TURNING

THE MIND

INTO AN

ALLY

Sakyong Mipham

While the author has made every effort to provide accurate
telephone numbers and Internet addresses at the time of
publication, neither the publisher nor the author assumes
any responsibility for errors, or for changes that occur
after publication.

RIVERHEAD BOOKS
a member of
Penguin Putnam Inc.
375 Hudson Street
New York, NY 10014

Traditional verses on p. 213 translated by the Nālandā
Translation Committee. Used by permission.

Library of Congress Cataloging-in-Publication Data

Sakyong Mipham Rinpoche, date.
Turning the mind into an ally / Sakyong Mipham.
p.   cm.
ISBN 1-57322-206-2
1. Meditation—Buddhism. 2. Spiritual life—
Buddhism. I. Title
BQ5612 .S24 2003   2002067961
294.3'4435—dc21

Printed in the United States of America
1   3   5   7   9   10   8   6   4   2

This book is printed on acid-free paper. ∞

Book design by Jennifer Ann Daddio

To my father and mother,

CHÖGYAM TRUNGPA RINPOCHE

and

LADY KUNCHOK PALDEN

ACKNOWLEDGMENTS

I am grateful to the Vidyadhara Chögyam Trungpa Rinpoche—my father, my teacher, and my best friend; His Holiness Dilgo Khyentse Rinpoche for guiding and inspiring me through challenging times; His Holiness Penor Rinpoche for his total support and blessings; Khenpo Namdrol for his teaching and wisdom; and Lama Pegyal, Loppön Rechung, and Loppön Gawang for their support and enthusiasm. Thanks to David Schneider for his original encouragement; Samuel Bercholz and Jonathan Green for their advice; Joe Spieler for helping me in the process; Amy Hertz for her vision, energy, and patience; and Pema Chödrön for her foreword. For their friendship and support, thanks to Lucas Dayley, Molly McCue, Judith Outlaw, and Rose Taylor. I also extend appreciation to all the people who have transcribed and edited my talks over the years.

For their generosity and daring, I thank Mark Butler, Wells Christie, Jeff Cohn and Jane Carpenter Cohn, Neal Greenberg, James and Sharon Hoagland, and in particular, Amy Bajakian, who offered me her home to work in whenever I wanted to. I appreciate the personal support of Douglas Anderson, Barry Boyce, David Brown, Dinah Brown, David Cook, Susan Dreier, David Ellerton, Jesse Grimes, Richard Hartman, Kevin Hoagland, Noel McLellan, Joe Mauricio, John Sennhauser, Ken Sussman, and Mark Thorpe.

Most of all, I want to thank Emily Bower and Elizabeth Monson for their tireless, endless hours of helping; Mark Matousek for his good intention and hard work; Jules Levinson for his advice, insight, continuous support, and encouragement; and Adam Lobel for his encouragement and enthusiasm. For auspicious coincidence, my gratitude to Emily Hilburn Sell. We met at the right time in the right place, and without this connection the book would not have materialized.

CONTENTS

∞

Three

TURNING THE MIND
INTO AN ALLY

Four

WARRIOR IN THE WORLD

FOREWORD

I first met Sakyong Mipham Rinpoche years ago in Boulder, Colorado, through his father, my teacher Chögyam Trungpa Rinpoche. He and the Sakyong's mother, Lady Kunchok Palden, were among the survivors of a refugee group that had narrowly escaped from Tibet to India in 1959. Trungpa Rinpoche, who had been the supreme abbot of the Surmang monasteries, was descended from the warrior king Gesar, a historical figure who is a pivotal source of the Shambhala teachings. Before Sakyong Mipham was born, his father predicted that he would be a very special child, that his early years would be difficult, and that he would emerge as a great teacher. He then requested that Lady Kunchok bless their unborn son by making a pilgrimage to all the sacred Buddhist sites throughout India. When she reached Bodhgaya, the place of the Buddha's enlightenment, the Sakyong apparently decided to arrive. He was born at this holiest of Buddhist sites in December 1962.

During his earliest years, Sakyong Mipham lived with his mother in Tibetan refugee villages in northwest India. His father sent for him to join him in the West at the age of eight. When Sakyong Mipham was a teenager, I became his meditation instructor at Trungpa Rinpoche's request. Looking back, I realize that my teacher was purposely deepening my bond with his son. Every week I would meet with the Sakyong to discuss his meditation. After only a few months, however, I realized that our roles had reversed. The young Sakyong was now instructing me. The relationship that was set in motion back then has only deepened over the years. At the same time, I've watched a somewhat reticent youth grow into a courageous, confident, and wise teacher who is of enormous benefit to his many students throughout the world.

In 1979 Trungpa Rinpoche privately empowered the Sakyong as his heir and began to guide and instruct him even more closely than before. On a day shortly before this event, Rinpoche said to me, "You aren't going to make my son into a monk, are you? Because I have very different plans for him."

These plans began to come to complete fruition after Trungpa Rinpoche died in 1987, when Sakyong

Mipham took over leadership of his father's Shambhala Buddhist community. Later he was recognized by His Holiness Penor Rinpoche as the rebirth of the nineteenth-century meditation master and scholar Mipham Jamyang Gyatso, one of the most renowned teachers in Tibetan Buddhism. At the same time he was enthroned as the Sakyong ("earth protector"), head of the Shambhala lineage.

After years of training with his father as well as undergoing a Western education, the Sakyong now returned to Asia to further deepen his meditation and studies under the tutelage of His Holiness Dilgo Khyentse Rinpoche and His Holiness Penor Rinpoche, two of the greatest Tibetan Buddhist masters. It is remarkable to me how natural it was for him to start to speak Tibetan again and to step back into the Tibetan way of thinking. One day I asked him how it was that his grasp of the most profound, often extremely difficult Buddhist teachings came so easily to him. He said, "Well, it seems so familiar, as if I'm just remembering it all." He continues to travel to India every year. He says that he's never happier than when he's doing this study.

Here we have a teacher with a remarkable ability to digest the traditional Tibetan Buddhist teachings thoroughly and completely and then present them in a way that speaks directly to the hearts and needs of Western people. Moreover, his enthusiasm for doing this is contagious. As one who is now completely at home in both the Western and Tibetan mind-sets, he easily and spontaneously serves as a bridge.

In 2001 Sakyong Mipham visited Tibet for the first time, where he was greeted by thousands of people, not only as the current Sakyong and the rebirth of Mipham, but also as living proof of the vitality of Buddhism, returning to the place that his father had left. Huge audiences gathered to hear his teachings.

This book is the ideal next step in Sakyong Mipham's journey, as it introduces him to a world sorely in need of the traditional mind-training practices he presents. The beauty of his approach is that it joins two streams of teachings: Buddhism and Shambhala, a spiritual warriorship grounded in realization of basic goodness. Here Sakyong Mipham offers detailed instructions for building a courageous mind through the practice of sitting meditation, the natural seat of the warrior bodhisattva. A skilled equestrian, he compares the whole process to taming a wild horse. He generously includes descriptions of the obstacles we might encounter in such rigorous work, along with the antidotes traditionally prescribed by the lineage of Tibetan and Indian meditators.

In addition, Sakyong Mipham instructs the reader in contemplative meditation, which sharpens our insight and develops our wisdom. Contemplation provides the conditions for joy to expand as we realize the nature of reality. He places particular emphasis on the practice of rousing *bodhichitta*—awakened heart—an enlightened strategy through which we begin to experience our great warrior spirit.

It is difficult to believe that the boy I met so many years ago is the exuberant and powerful teacher I study with today. Yet there is one thing that remains the same—his radiant, somewhat mischievous smile. When that young man smiled at me, I instantly felt love and a profound bond with him—a love and connection that I have felt ever since. That his teachings are finally available to a wider audience is wonderful. That they will benefit all who read them, I have no doubt. I am delighted that this book makes so available the clear and precise wisdom of my heart-friend and precious teacher, Sakyong Mipham Rinpoche.

—Pema Chödrön

PREFACE

Many of the people that I meet as I teach throughout the world are questioning what it means to be content and happy. So many feel that we've somehow wandered from our roots, from something very basic to our hearts and minds. The ramifications of this wandering are far-reaching, manifesting in psychological pain, acts of aggression, and consistent confusion about the nature of reality. For many of us, life is not leading toward awakening. In the Shambhala Buddhist tradition, we call this situation "the dark age."

It is in such times that we turn to spiritual teachings. We try to find something that can help us. But taking a spiritual path isn't meant to be just a way to deal with hard times. Following a spiritual path is how we awaken to our unique and precious power as humans. It can be a natural way of life in all situations, not just a way to feel better. We all have seeds inside us that we would like to nourish, which is why we yearn for deeper meaning in our lives.

When I'm teaching, people often ask me questions in hopes of hearing some esoteric truth. They seem to want me to tell them a secret. But the most fundamental secret I know is rooted in something that we already possess—basic goodness. In spite of the extreme hardship and cruelty we see happening throughout the world, the basis of everything is completely pure and good. Our heart and mind are inherently awake. This basic goodness is a quality of complete wholesomeness. It includes everything. But before we can begin the adventure of transforming ourselves into awakened people—much less the adventure of living our lives with true joy and happiness—we need to discover this secret for ourselves. Then we have the real possibility of cultivating courage, from which we can radiate love and compassion to others.

My father, Chögyam Trungpa—who was also my teacher—was a pioneer in introducing Tibetan Buddhism in the West. He also introduced the teachings of Shambhala, a legendary enlightened society. The first king of Shambhala received teachings directly from the Buddha. The story goes that everyone in the kingdom of Shambhala then began to practice meditation and care for others by generating love and compassion.

Shambhala became a peaceful, prosperous place where rulers and subjects alike were wise and kind.

No one really knows whether the kingdom of Shambhala still exists. But if we think of it as the root of wakefulness and brilliant sanity that lives within each of us, it still has the possibility to uplift us, both personally and as a society. The way we reach this kingdom is by discovering basic goodness for ourselves. Then we can cultivate love and compassion. The first step is to train our minds through meditation. For dealing with the rigors of life, the mind of meditation is a wonderful ally.

One

WHY

MEDITATE?

One

The Rock and
the Flower

Many of us are slaves to our minds. Our own mind is our worst enemy. We try to focus, and our mind wanders off. We try to keep stress at bay, but anxiety keeps us awake at night. We try to be good to the people we love, but then we forget and put ourselves first. And when we want to change our life, we dive into spiritual practice and expect to see quick results, only to lose focus after the honeymoon has worn off. We return to our state of bewilderment. We're left feeling helpless and discouraged.

It seems we all agree that training the body through exercise, diet, and relaxation is a good idea, but why don't we think about training our mind? Working with our mind and emotional states can help us in any activity in which we engage, whether it's sports or business or study—or a religious path. I've been riding most of my life, for example, and I love horses. When riding a horse, you have to be awake and aware of what you are doing each moment. The horse is alive and expecting communication, and you have to be sensitive to its mood. To space out could be dangerous.

Once when I was staying with friends in Colorado, I took one of my favorite horses, Rocky, on a trail ride through some back country. I had ridden Rocky before, mostly in the arena. He was very intelligent, but he didn't know how to walk a trail. This was a new situation. I was leading the group, and that also made him a little nervous. I coaxed him over certain rocks and shifted my weight to indicate to him to go around certain others, but he kept stumbling.

We came to a narrow place in the trail. On one side was a steep shale cliff and on the other, a long drop into a river. Rocky stopped and waited for my direction. We both knew that one wrong move would plummet us into the river below. I guided him toward the gorge, subtly shifting my weight toward the high wall of shale. I thought that if he slipped, I could jump off and save myself.

The moment I shifted, Rocky stopped cold and craned his head around to look at me. He knew exactly what I was doing. I could tell that he was shocked and hurt that I was planning to abandon him. The look in his eye said, "You and me together, right?" Seeing how terrified he was, I shifted my weight back. He swung his head forward in relief and we negotiated the trail together with no problems.

On that ride, Rocky and I created a synergistic bond, a wordless rapport. It's that kind of connection that I think we can all have with our own minds. In *shamatha* meditation—"peaceful abiding"—we train our minds in stability, clarity, and strength. Through this most basic form of sitting meditation, we discover that we can abide peacefully. Knowing our natural peace is the basis for any spiritual path—the beginning and the ground for anyone courageous enough to seek true happiness. It is the first step to becoming a buddha, which literally means "awakened one." We all have the potential to awaken from the sleep of ignorance to the truth of reality.

Training our mind through peaceful abiding, we can create an alliance that allows us to actually use our mind, rather than be used by it. This is a practice that anyone can do. Although it has its roots in Buddhism, it is a complement to any spiritual tradition. If we want to undo our own bewilderment and suffering and be of benefit to others and the planet, we're going to have to be responsible for learning what our own mind is and how it works, no matter what beliefs we hold. Once we see how our mind works, we see how our life works, too. That changes us.

That's the point of talking about mind and meditation. The more we understand about ourselves and how our mind works, the more the mind *can* work. The Tibetan *lesu rungwa* means that the mind is functional. My father used to sometimes translate this as "workable." It means that we can train the mind to work in order to use it to do something particular. For example, if we want to generate compassion and love, that's work.

There is an old saying that bringing Buddhism to a new culture is like bringing a flower and a rock together. The flower represents the potential for compassion and wisdom, clarity and joy to blossom in our life. The rock represents the solidity of a bewildered mind. If we want the flower to take root and grow, we have to work to create the right conditions. The way to do this—both as individuals and as people in a culture in which the attainment of personal comfort sometimes seems to be the highest standard—is to soften up our hearts, our minds, our lives. True happiness is always available to us, but first we have to create the environment for it to flourish.

We might have a deep aspiration to slow down, to be more compassionate, to be fearless, to live with confidence and dignity, but we're often not able to accomplish these things because we're so set in our ways. Our minds seem so inflexible. We've been touched by the softness of the flower, but we haven't figured out how to make a place for it. We may feel that our ability to love or feel compassion is limited, and that that's just the way things are.

The problem for most of us is that we're trying to grow a flower on a rock. The garden hasn't been tilled properly. We haven't trained our minds. It doesn't work to just throw some seeds on top of the hard ground and then hope for the flowers to grow. We have to prepare the ground, which requires effort. First we have to move the rocks and hoe the weeds. Then we have to soften up the earth and create nice topsoil. This is what we're doing by learning to peacefully abide in sitting meditation: creating the space for our garden to grow. Then we can cultivate qualities that will allow us to live our lives in full bloom.

A society of hard and inflexible minds is a society that is incapable of nurturing the flowers of love and compassion. This is the source of the dark age. We tend to question our goodness and our wisdom. When we question these things, we begin to use seemingly more convenient ways to deal with our problems. We are less ready to use love and compassion, more ready to use aggression. So we have to continuously remind ourselves of basic goodness. If we want to help alleviate suffering on our planet, those of us who can make our minds pliable must plant a flower on the rock. This is how we can create a society based on the energy we get from experiencing our own basic goodness. In Tibet we call this energy *lungta*, "windhorse."

It is important to look at what actually works, what inspires people to meditate, to study, and to put the teachings into effect. As a lifelong student of meditation, I have a deep respect for its profundity as a spiritual path. I am interested in what people can really use in their life, and how to prepare people to truly hear the potency and depth of what an enlightened being like the Buddha has to say. I am grateful to my teachers for passing these teachings on to me, and grateful for the chance to share them with you.

The teachings are always available, like a radio signal in the air. But a student needs to learn how to tune in to that signal, and how to stay tuned in. We can begin the process of personal development now by including short periods of meditation as part of our everyday lives. Tilling the ground of our own minds through meditation is how we begin to create a community garden. In doing so we are helping to create a new culture, a culture that can thrive in the modern world and can at the same time support our human journey in an uplifted and joyous way. Such a culture is called enlightened society. Enlightened society is where the flower and the rock will meet.

Two

Bewilderment and
Suffering

My father and mother were born in Tibet, but I was
born in India and didn't visit my parents' native land
until 2001. When I was in Tibet, I traveled through
some of the most vast, spacious, and beautiful land in
the world. Our caravan of land-cruisers drove through
remote valleys surrounded by endless mountain ranges.
For mile after mile we would pass no sign of civiliza-
tion. There were, of course, no bathrooms, so we would
stop to relieve ourselves along the side of the road. No
matter how isolated we thought we were, someone
would always come walking around the bend. Then
another person would come close to check out this
strange group of travelers in his valley. By the time we
stood there for more than a minute, the equivalent of
a whole village would have gathered, laughing and

smiling and staring into our vehicles. I wondered where they were coming from and where they were going. I would think, "Are they born from the earth?" Probably they were just heading for another herd of yaks or a distant monastery, or simply moving to a warmer place. They each had a destination.

The simplicity of that environment made it so clear that this is what most of us are doing: traveling from one place to another, searching for a lasting happiness. There's an element of emptiness that we keep trying to assuage. We want to find something that feels good and makes sense, something solid that we can use as a permanent reference point. Wisdom might tell us that we're seeking something we won't ever find, yet part of the reason we keep looking is that we've never quite been satisfied. Even when we feel great happiness, there's a quality of intangibility, as if we're squeezing a watermelon seed. Yet day in and day out, year after year, and, according to traditional Buddhism, lifetime after lifetime, we don't think beyond accomplishing the immediate desire to find the missing piece, the one that will bring us real happiness.

Since I'm a Buddhist, the Buddha is my role model for an enlightened being. He was a strong person with a healthy sense of self—a caring, clear-minded individual in harmony with himself and his environment. He saw how much suffering was present in the world, and he wanted to help. After following many different spiritual paths, he developed the strength, confidence, and motivation that he needed to meditate and rest in wisdom. This is how he awoke to the deepest meaning of reality and was able endlessly to help others do the same. He was a bodhisattva warrior—one who cultivates compassion and wisdom, who has the courage to live from the open heart. His journey shows us that we too can arouse our open hearts as a way to realize the meaning of being fully human.

The Buddha was born a prince. Because he seemed to have a spiritual bent, his father decided early on that it would be better for him not to get too curious about the world outside the walls of the palace. He didn't want his only son going out to seek his spiritual fortune, which was a popular thing to do in India back then. So the king kept the world within the royal walls humming with all kinds of entertainment, activities, and sensual delights. The Buddha grew up with everything he needed, all within the walls of his own private world. When he was older, there were dancing girls and later a wife and baby. For a long time, he didn't get to know the world beyond the walls. But then one day he rode out with a servant and saw sick people, old people, dead people, and a wandering ascetic. This completely changed his view. No longer could he live to simply take delight in the entertainments of the royal world, where his father had managed to keep from him the facts of life. His father's worst fears came true, and the Buddha left the kingdom immediately. Dissatisfied with maintaining an illusion, he wanted to understand his life — and life itself. Just like the Buddha, most of us also would like to learn some basic truth about our lives and get a bigger perspective about what's going on. The path of meditation offers us this possibility.

What the Buddha saw is that life is marked by four qualities: impermanence, suffering, selflessness, and peace. He saw that we keep butting our heads against this basic reality and it hurts. We suffer because we want life to be different from what it is. We suffer because we try to make pleasurable what is painful, to make solid what is fluid, to make permanent what is always changing. The Buddha saw that we try to make ourselves into something real and unchanging when our fundamental state of being is unconditionally open and ungraspable — selfless. We discover this notion of selflessness in meditation, where we learn to zoom away from our thoughts and emotions and become familiar with these basic facts of life. Accepting the impermanence and selflessness of our existence, we will stop suffering and realize peace. That, in a nut-shell, is what the Buddha taught. It sounds simple. Yet instead of relaxing into this elemental truth, we keep searching around the next corner and never getting quite what we want. In Buddhist language, that is known as *samsara*. In Tibetan, the word is *khorwa*, which means "circular."

Samsara is a circle of suffering, like a wheel that endlessly goes around and around. We are spinning our wheels. We keep looking for something to be different. Next time we will be happy. This relationship didn't work out—but the next one will. This restaurant isn't that good—but the next item on the menu might really do it for me. My last meditation session wasn't great, and the one before that wasn't great either—but this one's really going to be different. One thing keeps leading to another, and instead of the simplicity and happiness we desire, we only feel more burdened by our lives. Instead of relaxing into the basic goodness that connects us with every other living being, we suffer the illness of separation, which is just a trick of our minds.

The Buddha said, "True suffering is the nature of samsara." We may not even see the suffering in our life, partly because we've become so accustomed to it. But if we look beneath the surface, we'll see that suffering is percolating through like an underground river. Whether we acknowledge it or not, we sense that it's there and maintain a mental vigilance to keep ourselves occupied in an attempt to avoid it. Over and over again we come up with schemes to outsmart samsara. Even though we know that nothing changes the basic character of samsara, we keep trying to make it work out. This is high-maintenance pleasure. It's what keeps us on the wheel. It's how we keep trying to make samsara work. We think, "I know it's endless. I know it's painful. I know what you're saying. I believe you. But I've got just one more thing, just one little thing." We can go to the grave saying this. That is samsara. "Just one more" is the binding factor of the cycle of suffering.

The Buddha was an astronaut who traveled into space and saw that suffering is a circle. We say "just one more" because we don't see it the way Buddha did. We're under the illusion that we're moving in a straight line. Yet just as the Earth seems flat as long as we're on it, we think we're walking in a straight line when actually we're stuck in a circle of suffering.

And though it certainly feels like an objective reality, this circle of suffering is just a state of mind. For example, we might think of a violent part of a big city as "samsaric." If the Buddha were in that place, however, he wouldn't experience it that way at all. He would experience it just as it is, without the filter of judgment or opinion. It's our mind that's samsaric. Suffering is the state of mind that regards itself as real. We can spend our whole life trying to create a solid, lasting self. We can spend our whole life looking outside ourselves for something to reflect this delusion of solidity, to be as real and lasting as we wish ourselves to be. Search though we will, it's impossible to find what doesn't exist, and the perpetual search causes suffering. The Buddha saw the reality that we're bewildered and suffering because we take ourselves so seriously. We haven't seen the open radiance of basic goodness, our natural state.

The fact is that what appears to us as a solid reality is actually in a state of continuous flux. The world is a continuous state of flux. The house that we grew up in is not the same house anymore. The mother and father that we knew when we were children are physically different now. Where is our first bicycle? At one time, it seemed so real. Everything is always coming together and falling apart, and it doesn't seem to pose a problem for anyone but us. Spring knows how to be summer and autumn leaves know how to fall down. Coming together and falling apart is the movement of time, the movement of life. This is as obvious as our own face, and yet we imagine our self as solid and unchanging. We stick up for it; we protect it. We feel angry when someone challenges the opinions we hold dear. If something doesn't go our way, we feel insulted. When something interrupts our routine, we feel a sense of loss. We try to ward off signs of aging.

The Buddha said, "I'm not going to tell you one way or another; but if you are real, then where are you? And if the world is real, then where is it?" In Buddhism we talk about emptiness because when we start to investigate that self, we can't find anything solid or substantial. There's a *sense* of self—a shadow. We have eyes and visual consciousness—that is a sense of "me." We have touch and feeling—that is a sense of "me." We have memories, thoughts, actions, and speech, all adding up to a sense of "me." We have a body and the pleasure and pain that come with that, and those things are "me," too. This sense of self is mentally fabricated, defined by outer conditions. We say, "I don't feel like myself today." But when we look for this self that we want to feel like—where is it? The same is true for the world around us. We feel that everything is just as it appears. Yet if we look beneath the surface, we find that our universe is not quite as stable as it seems. The things "out there" change just as much as we do.

With this kind of practice and inquisitiveness, an enlightened being like the Buddha learns to look at the landscape of life in a clear, unbiased way. When he began to teach, the Buddha was just reporting his observations: "This is what I see about how things are." He wasn't presenting any particular viewpoint. He wasn't preaching dogma; he was pointing out reality. Saying that impermanence is a Buddhist belief is like saying that Buddhists believe water is wet. The Buddha didn't create impermanence or selflessness, suffering or peace; the Buddha just saw reality, noticed how it works, and acknowledged it for the rest of us. We can spend our entire life trying to create a solid self, but we won't be able to make it stick. Once we relax into this simple truth, we can go beyond bewilderment and suffering.

I recently had an amusing experience with a Tibetan lama friend. He had just arrived in the West for the first time, and I was having fun showing him different aspects of our culture. He's a learned man, but when it came to his adventure in discovering the ways of the West, he was very innocent. I took him to see the film *The Grinch,* thinking that although he couldn't understand all the dialogue, at least it would be colorful and entertaining for him, and he would enjoy the special effects.

We watched the movie and he seemed to like it. Afterward, I asked him if he understood it. He said, "Just one question: What is Christmas?" I answered that it's the holiday celebrating the birth of Jesus Christ. Then he said in a very respectful tone of voice, "So, that green monkey in the movie was Jesus Christ?"

I had a good laugh over that, especially because he was being so respectful. I realized that as bizarre as his question sounded, it was genuine. I asked, "Why do you think that?"

"Well, he lived in a cave in the mountains and he had a rough time in the beginning, and then things got better, and in the end it all seemed good."

In Tibet, many of the historical and mythical holy people live in caves and are eccentric. There is a famous saintlike yogi named Milarepa who lived in a cave in the mountains. He had all kinds of adventures and overcame incredible obstacles through meditation. During his years in the cave, he lived on nettle soup much of the time, and it is said that his skin turned green. In addition, Tibetan mythology has it that humans are partly descended from monkeys.

My friend was pulling together different ideas from his experience to draw his strange conclusion. He was making a leap from his culture into ours. And of course, it seems absurd to us that anyone would think that the Grinch was Jesus Christ. It's just as absurd to think we have a self. Yet we spend our lives clinging to an imaginary identity cobbled together from different thoughts and concepts, trying to keep it happy, and that is why we suffer. This isn't a sin, it's an ancient habit perpetuated by our bewildered minds.

The bewildered mind is like a wild horse. It runs away when we try to find it, shies when we try to approach it. If we find a way to ride it, it takes off with the bit in its teeth and finally throws us right into the mud. We think that the only way to steady it is to give it what it wants. We spend so much of our energy trying to satisfy and entertain this wild horse of a mind.

The bewildered mind is weak because it is continually distracted. It's distracted by the overriding need to maintain the comfort of "me." It is meditating on discursiveness and self-absorption and that leads to suffering, because the bewildered mind can't go beyond itself. When difficulty arises, it's unable to cope. When the unexpected occurs, it reacts from the limited perspective of wanting to stay happy in a small place. So if we're threatened, we strike out with anger. If somebody has something we want, automatically we feel jealous. If we see something we like, we feel desire. We might not question these responses—not even ask, "Is it worth getting angry about?" What makes us happy and what makes us sad come down to volatile outer conditions, circumstances that are constantly changing. This adds up to bewilderment and suffering for us.

With an untrained mind, we'll live most days of our lives at the mercy of our moods. Waking up in the morning is like gambling: "What mind did I end up with today? Is it the irritated mind, the happy mind, the anxious mind, the angry mind, the compassionate mind, or the loving mind?" Most of the time we believe that the mind-set we have is who we are and we live our day from it. We meditate on it. We don't question it. Whether we wake up feeling dread or excitement or just feeling sleepy, the propelling motivation is simply wanting things to go well for "me."

There's a place between Earth and Mars that scientists call the Goldilocks zone. It's a place that's not too hot, not too cold, but *just right*—a place where life could conceivably be supported. Many of us live from the motivation to keep ourselves in such a zone. We spend our lives constructing a personal Goldilocks zone where our solid sense of self feels comfortable and protected. Everything's just how we like it, and we work to keep it that way.

Perpetuating this zone involves worrying. Many different aspects of our life must align in order for us to be happy. If they don't come together, we're going to suffer. Our mind chews on hope and fear because it's unable to relax. We're afraid of what will happen if we loosen our grip on ourselves. So we continually spin a web of concepts, beliefs, opinions, and moods that we identify as "me." It's like a closed-circuit TV. We're always sure of where we are; there's not much else to be known; nothing will ever really touch us. We work to draw in what will make us happy, fend off whatever causes pain, and pretty much ignore the rest. This is what most of us consider pleasure. We create a comfort zone based on the motivation "I just want to get by." I call this the "have a nice day" approach.

As a motivation for living our lives, "have a nice day" is very confining. It keeps us trapped in dissatisfaction, self-involvement, and fear. We feel defensive and claustrophobic. We are running on speed, need, and greed. And we are often moving so quickly that we don't even notice that we *have* a motivation. That sense of oppression is maintained by our bewildered, untrained mind. It's all-pervasive, deep, as if we're dreaming. This is suffering.

There is a different approach to our lives. We can wake up to our enlightened qualities: unconditional love and compassion; uninhibited, total ease with ourselves; a clear and sharp mind. In order to open our courageous warrior heart, however, we first have to understand the nature of our bewilderment. What's going on in samsara, this cyclical existence that entraps us? From the Buddhist point of view, we've created our own situation. We're operating out of a basic and habitual misunderstanding. Even though we're dreaming, we think we're real. No matter what we do to hold ourselves together, the truth is that we are always falling apart. As soon as we wash our car, it rains. So what are we going to do about it? The Buddha suggests that rather than resist samsara, complain about it, or keep trying to outsmart it, we take a good long look and say, "Let's figure out what's happening here."

We have to understand the suffering of our bewildered mind and decide that we've had enough of it. We're not fleeing from the world. Rather, we're recognizing the dreamlike quality of existence and not buying into it—or ourselves—as hard and real. Once we understand the play of impermanence and selflessness, we can take ourselves less seriously and enjoy life much more. If, like the Buddha, we were able to see the empty and luminous nature of reality, we'd wake up from our dream in a snap. True liberation is life without the illusion of "me"—or "you."

Just like the Buddha, however, we have to go on a journey before we can see reality so clearly. The journey begins with understanding why we suffer. We have to recognize the basic landscape we're living in. If our goal in life is to give "me" a good time, it won't work out. Why? Because the lay of the land is birth, aging, sickness, and death. That's the game plan for "me." And within that, we have pleasure that keeps changing into pain. There's no permanence or stability here, nor is there a solid self. Death comes, often without warning. We suffer when we spend our lives denying the basic truth of our existence.

Our human lives are exceedingly precious because they offer us the possibility of discovering our inherent awakeness. Like pictures we see of the Buddha, "awake" is shimmering, radiant, fluid, and primordially pure. It's what we're made of, and it connects us all. What lies between us and the joy of this basic goodness is the trick our bewildered minds keep playing. Meditation is how we unravel the illusion.

It's fine to take pleasure, to enjoy good food, and to listen to beautiful music. Becoming curious about how we suffer doesn't mean that we can no longer enjoy eating ice cream. But once we begin to understand the bewilderment of our untrained mind, we won't look to the ice cream and say, "That's happiness." We'll realize that the mind can be happy devoid of ice cream. We'll realize that the mind is content and happy by nature.

Three

Peaceful Abiding

Even though the bewildered mind is untrained, it is already meditating, whether we know it or not. Meditation is the natural process of becoming familiar with an object by repeatedly placing our minds upon it. Whatever we're doing, we always have a view; we're always placing our mind on one object or another. For example, when we get up in the morning and we're anxious about something, anxiety becomes our view for the day: "What about me? When will I get what I want?" The object of our meditation is "me."

In peaceful abiding, we ground our mind in the present moment. We place our mind on the breath and practice keeping it there. We notice when thoughts and emotions distract us, and train in continually returning our mind to the breath. This is how we shift our allegiance from the bewildered mind that causes its own suffering to the mind that is stable, clear, and strong. We proclaim our desire to discover this mind of stability, clarity, and strength by learning to rest in our own peace.

Turning the mind into an ally is a matter of learning to see ourselves as we are. Ordinarily we just can't handle the natural joy of our mind, so we end up churning up intense emotions. These emotions keep us trapped in suffering. In peaceful abiding we begin to see how the mind works.

"Peaceful abiding" describes the mind as it naturally is. The word *peace* tells the whole story. The human mind is by nature joyous, calm, and very clear. In shamatha meditation we aren't creating a peaceful state—we're letting our mind be as it is to begin with. This doesn't mean that we're peacefully ignoring things. It means that the mind is able to be in itself without constantly leaving.

From a Buddhist point of view, human beings aren't intrinsically aggressive; we are inherently peaceful. This is sometimes hard to believe. When we're angry or upset, our untrained mind becomes belligerent and we routinely strike out at others. We imagine that reacting aggressively to the object of our emotion will resolve our pain. Throughout history we have used this approach over and over again. Striking out when we're in pain is clearly one way we perpetuate misery.

With a trained mind, a stable mind, a mind with a larger motivation than its own comfort, we find another way to work with the difficulties of daily life. When we're in a difficult situation, we maintain our seat. Instead of perpetuating misery by acting out aggression, we learn to use the rough spots to spark the courage to proceed on our journey. Eventually we may actually be able to turn the mind of anger into the energy of love and compassion.

But first we learn how to abide peacefully. If we can remember what the word *shamatha* means, we can always use it as a reference point. We can say, "What is this meditation that I'm doing? It is calm, peaceful abiding." At the same time we'll begin to see that our mind is always abiding somewhere—not necessarily in its peaceful natural state. Perhaps it's abiding in irritation, anger, jealousy. Seeing all of this is how we begin to untangle our bewilderment.

We're accustomed to living a life based on running after our wild mind, a mind that is continually giving birth to thoughts and emotions. It's not that there's anything inherently wrong with thoughts and emotions— in fact, the point of making our mind an ally is that we can begin to direct them for benefit. Through peacefully abiding we begin to see our emotions at work. We begin to see that we have to work with these intense emotions because if we don't, they'll grow. Once they grow, we act on them. When we act on them, they create our environment.

Meditation shows how discursive thoughts lead to emotions — irritation, anxiety, passion, aggression, jealousy, pride, greed — which lead to suffering. For example, the person sitting next to you on the bus has a really fancy CD player. First you're intrigued by all the bells and whistles. Then, before you know it, you want one just like it, even though your own player was perfectly adequate two minutes ago. You were sitting there peacefully, and now you're a volcano of desire. On top of that, you're jealous of this total stranger for having something you want. You were enjoying the ride, and now, a few thoughts later, you're miserable.

Reacting to emotion creates further reactions later. We're planning a vacation with a friend and disagree about what day to leave. Our friend is angry, which makes us angry, which makes him angrier, and before we know it, our trip is down the drain. Being discursive might feel good, just as food we're allergic to tastes good, but after we eat it, we suffer.

Meditation is a very personal journey. Simply by being conscious of the present moment so we can ground ourselves in it, we relax our sense of self and begin to tune in to reality as it is. We begin to realize what we don't know, and we become curious: "What is truly valid? What is the truth of my experience?" If we lived in the wilderness, we'd observe nature's patterns around us: the activity of the birds and animals, the behavior of the weather, and changes in the plant life. After a while, we'd be intimate with the environment. We might be able to predict when winter is coming and whether it would be long or short. Similarly, in peaceful abiding we can begin to observe and understand our thought patterns. We can watch how our mind weaves from one idea to another, one emotion to another. We can see how it fabricates a comfort zone. We can see how it wants to take action. We can begin to understand its course without judging it. We just notice the internal environment and become familiar with it.

After we've spent some time watching thoughts and emotions come and go, we begin to see them clearly. They no longer have the power to destabilize us, because we see how ephemeral they are. Then we can actually begin to change our patterns, and in doing so, change our whole environment. But to reap this benefit requires consistent practice.

Once we establish a regular practice, our life can feel like it's undergoing a major upheaval. Meditating is a new way of looking at things. We have to be willing to change. When we begin to tame the movement of our mind, it affects everything else. It's like renovating: once you start, it's hard to stop. For example, at

Shambhala Mountain Center, where I teach every summer, our meditation hall was getting old and funky, so we built a new one. Then by contrast, the kitchen looked small and old, so we needed to build a new kitchen, too.

In beginning to meditate, you might see things about yourself that you don't like, so it's important to ask yourself if you're willing to change. Before you consider entering a spiritual path, you have to begin by looking at the basic ground. Before you even sit down, ask yourself these questions: Do I actually want to become a better person? Do I really want to work with my mind? We're not talking about becoming a goody-goody. We're saying that we can choose to become stronger, kinder, wiser, and more focused. We can become more in tune with how things are. Do we really want to do that?

The notion of meditation is very simple. We slow down and begin to look at the pattern of our life. We have to start with the mind, then the body follows. This is not to say that once we start meditating, everything will work out and we'll have no problems. We'll still have disagreements with friends and family, we'll still get parking tickets, we'll still miss flights, we'll still burn the toast on occasion. Meditation doesn't take us to the end of the rainbow—it opens the possibility of completely embodying our enlightened qualities by making our mind an ally. When we meditate, we're training ourselves to see our weak points and strengthen our positive ones. We're altering our basic perception. We're beginning to change how we relate to the world—but not forcefully.

Once we start really looking at the mind, we see some elements of how it works. For one, the mind is always placing itself on something. It has to do this in order to know what's going on. Generally we ingrain the tendency to follow distractions—which is the opposite of stabilizing the mind. Maybe the mind places itself on the idea of dinner. Then we think about what's in the refrigerator. Then we think about a restaurant. Then we think about what we'd wear to the restaurant. Then we think about buying new clothes. The mind is continually placing itself, usually for only a few seconds at a time. That is the case even when we're thinking systematically about something, such as a plan.

For instance, if I'm going from New York to Paris, I think about how I am going to do that. What day will I fly, at what time? Will I get frequent-flier miles? How long will it take? Then where will I go? And who will I see when I get there? If we look at our mind as it's planning, we'll see that between all those planning thoughts, other thoughts are arising. Although it may seem as if we're having a stream of thoughts about our vacation, if we look closely, we'll see that the mind is continuously bouncing back and forth between many thoughts—"It feels warm in here; shall I open a window? I wonder what's for lunch. Is there time to pick something up at the grocery store before the meeting this afternoon?" But since *most* of the thoughts are about the trip, we say, "Oh, I am planning my vacation."

Something else we'll see when we begin to look at our mind carefully is that we don't really perceive several things at once; we can only perceive one thing at a time. Try it out. It feels as if we hear the bird and see the sunshine at the same time, but in terms of the actual experience, the mind is moving from one perception to another. If we're thinking about what we are cooking for dinner, we'll have consecutive thoughts about it; in between, our mind places itself on other things many times over. The memory of a pleasant telephone encounter earlier in the day pops up; we notice that someone has washed the breakfast dishes; we like this track on the CD and we wonder who's singing. If we look closely at our mind, we see that it always behaves this way.

If we have enough similar thoughts, we call it a stream of consciousness, a stream of thought. However, the current of the mind is always fluctuating. The mind weaves an illusion of solidity by putting things together; it's actually going back and forth. At the beginning of peaceful abiding we discover what the mind is by drawing it in. We do this by sitting still and training in holding it to something for more than a few seconds. Repeatedly bringing it back to the breath may feel unnatural at the beginning, like having to hold a child to keep him from squirming. But if we keep doing it, at some point we begin to see that underneath the distraction and bewilderment, something else is going on. We begin to see the mind's underlying stillness. There is intelligence; there's some kind of stability; there's some kind of strength. We begin to see how the discursiveness of thoughts and emotions keeps us from experiencing these natural qualities of the mind.

In peaceful abiding we use the present moment as a reference point for relating to our mind and overcoming its wildness and discursiveness. When we sit down to meditate, there's so much going on in our mind that it's easy to get lost. We wander around in this dense jungle, not knowing where we are going. The present moment and the breath are like a hilltop in the distance. We keep our eyes on it as we walk toward it. We need to get to the hilltop, climb it, and look around so that we can figure out where we are.

Returning our mind to the breath is how we learn to be mindful and aware. It's like giving a child a pet: caring for a living creature teaches us responsibility and loving-kindness. When we grow up, we can express what we have learned to others. In the same way, we are using the breath as a vehicle to bring us into the present moment.

When I was young, I trained falcons. I would use tiny pieces of meat as a reference point. After a while, whenever I blew a whistle the bird would fly over to take the meat from my hand. It was challenging work, since the birds' natural tendency is not to trust a human. Training them for many months in captivity taught me the value of accepting small improvements day by day. After the trust was there, I could release the bird into the wild. That was the moment of truth: when I blew the whistle, would the bird return to my hand? This is very much like how we train our minds to return to the breath in peaceful abiding. It takes patience.

When we experience a moment of peacefully abiding, it seems so far-out. Our mind is no longer drifting, thinking about a million things. The sun comes up or a beautiful breeze comes along—and all of a sudden we feel the breeze and we are completely in tune. We think, "That's a very spiritual experience. It's a religious experience. At least worth a poem, or a letter home." But all that's happening is that for a moment we're in tune with our mind. Our mind is present and harmonious. Before, we were so busy and bewildered that we didn't even notice the breeze. Our mind couldn't even stay put long enough to watch the sun come up, which takes two and a half minutes. Now we can keep it in one place long enough to acknowledge and appreciate our surroundings. Now we are really here. In fact, being in the present moment is ordinary; it's the point of being human.

Learning to be present for the moment is the beginning of the spiritual path. By sitting still and training our mind to be with the breath, we begin to relax our discursiveness. We see how the mind creates our solid sense of self and begin to discover the mind's natural state of being. With this experience, we can cultivate our garden. The flowers of love, compassion, and wisdom gradually take over, and the weeds of anger, jealousy, and self-involvement have less and less room to grow. In peaceful abiding we become familiar with the ground of basic goodness. This is how we turn the mind into an ally.

Two

THE ART OF
PEACEFULLY
ABIDING

Four

Taking Our Seat

When I was a teenager, I would sometimes go on retreat with my father. On one retreat my practice consisted of four sessions of sitting meditation per day. My father would always sneak into my meditation room at the beginning of my session to see if I was beginning properly. I used to think, "Why doesn't he sneak in during the middle of my session, to see if I'm maintaining my practice?" After a while I realized that he was interested in how I was taking my seat. He was watching to see if I had the appropriate attitude toward training my mind. The mind is the king and queen. We approach our meditation seat as if it were a throne in the center of our life.

There are many statues and paintings of the Buddha in meditation posture. These beautifully illustrate how the posture is designed to allow natural strength and groundedness with some kind of openness and dignity. By taking an upright sitting posture, we enable the body to relax and the mind to be awake. You can use different postures for meditation, but under ordinary circumstances, sitting on either a cushion or a chair is best. If you're unable to sit, it is possible to do this technique while walking or standing or even lying down. However, the most efficient posture for this practice is sitting.

When you sit down, take a balanced, grounded posture to allow the energy in the center of your body to move freely. If you're on a cushion, sit with your legs loosely crossed. If you're in a chair, keep your legs uncrossed and your feet flat on the floor. Imagine that a string attached to the top of your head is pulling you upright. Let your organs, muscles, and bones settle around your erect spine, like a coat falling around a hanger. Your vertebrae should feel as though they are stacked like gold coins, allowing for the natural curvature of the spine.

When I was young, I would sit around comparing battle scars with a friend of mine who was also an incarnate lama. An incarnate lama is an individual who purposely takes a rebirth in a recognized lineage of teachers in order to continue working for the benefit of others. In the Tibetan tradition, this involves intensive, highly disciplined training. My tutor used to pinch me or use a bamboo switch, but my friend's tutor was more extreme. He taught his charge to hold his meditation posture by making him sit for hours on a rock surrounded by thorn bushes. If he moved, he'd be stuck with thorns. Although it sounds harsh, it was effective in teaching him to sit very still and upright.

The reason these tutors put so much emphasis on sitting up straight is that slouching impairs the breathing, which directly affects the mind. If you slump, you'll be struggling with discomfort in your body at the same time that you're trying to train your mind. What you want to be doing is the opposite: synchronizing your body and mind.

After you work with getting your spine straight, place your hands on your thighs. They shouldn't rest so far forward that it begins to pull your shoulders down, nor so far back that the shoulders contract and pinch the spine. The fingers are close and relaxed—not spread out in a grip, as if you can't let yourself go.

Tuck your chin in and relax your jaw. The tongue is also relaxed, the tip resting against your upper teeth. Your mouth is ever so slightly open. Your gaze is downward with the eyelids half shut. If the gaze takes in too much, it will be hard to abide peacefully. On the other hand, closing the eyes completely might encourage you to fall asleep or to withdraw your mind from the technique. If your mind feels removed and insular, intense and dark, try raising the gaze and allowing more space into your practice. The eyes aren't looking, by the way; the eyes just see. It is the same with sound—we aren't listening, but we do hear. In other words, we're not focusing with our senses.

The first step of the meditation technique is placement: placing our mind on the object of meditation. One of the Tibetan words for meditation is *gom,* which means "to become familiar with." In meditation we are introduced to an object and become familiar with it. We could use any object—a pebble, a flame, or the body. Our usual object of meditation—and the mind is always meditating on something—is "me."

In peaceful abiding, the object is the simple act of breathing. The breath represents being alive in the immediacy of the moment. Placing the mind on the breath and returning to it again and again is the essence of shamatha. Through resting the mind on the breath we stay present, awake, and mindful. Placement means staying with the feeling of the breathing. The flow of the breath soothes the mind and allows for steadiness and relaxation. It also reduces discursiveness.

This is ordinary breathing; nothing is exaggerated. We just breathe. If you're having a hard time staying with the breath—spacing out or losing track between breathing out and breathing in—counting the in- and out-cycles of the breath can be a helpful remedy to bring yourself back to focus. We breathe in, and then out — one. In and then out — two. If you use this method, count seven or twenty-one breaths and then start over. If you become distracted and lose count, start over again at one. Once you are more focused, you can drop the counting.

Becoming familiar with the subtle rhythms of the breath is part of the natural development of peaceful abiding. We're placing the mind on the whole breath, and it takes time to feel what that is. We might discover that the breath itself is not as solid as our concept of the breath. We might see that the word *breath* describes something that is not so much one entity as a series of events. Air enters through the nostrils, the abdomen expands, and the breath rests there for a moment. Then the diaphragm contracts and the breath leaves the lungs, gently exits the nostrils, and dissolves into space.

Using the breath as our object of meditation is very good because the air moving in and out allows us to have some kind of steadiness in contrast with our discursiveness. It also allows us to relax. That is the virtue of the breathing. Through placing our mind on this process, we relax our whole being. Tensions begin to dissolve. The breathing soothes the mind and allows it to rest. As our thoughts slow down and we settle into ourselves, the division between mind and body lessens. We start to feel our heart beating. We sense the flow of our blood. We can almost feel our bones. We become a whole being, with a synchronized body and mind.

But that's not all that's happening. As we sit and place our mind on the breath, the natural playfulness of the mind continually arises. The movement of thoughts and emotions distracts us. We tend to get lost in the flood. We're thinking about how interesting it is that we're finally meditating, and wonder what our friends will think. We're thinking about where we parked the car. We're thinking about how good a cookie would taste right now. We're thinking that we're sleepy and could use a cup of coffee. These thoughts are little stories we're telling ourselves. Most of them concern the past and future, not the present.

We may become swept away for a while and forget that the breath — not the thoughts and emotions — is the object of our meditation. The technique at this point is that when we notice that we're thinking, we acknowledge it. We can label it if we wish — "Thinking." Whether we label it or not, when we notice it, we bring our minds back to the breath. In acknowledging thoughts, we're recognizing the movement of the mind, the wildness of the bewildered mind. We're training in awareness of who we are as human beings. We're training in being undistracted and focused. We're training in being fully present for our lives.

For example, we're holding a sturdy and relaxed posture and have placed our mind on the breath. We relax into the breathing and are in the midst of peacefully resting our mind when a thought pops up: "I hope I don't have to cook again tonight. Why doesn't anyone else cook dinner? I'm the only one in the house who's really working anymore. Who do they think I am, Superman?" Our peaceful abiding has been flooded by a current of thinking that is about to become an emotional torrent. At some point, we see this. "Oh! I'm thinking." Acknowledging it, we allow the thought to dissipate, and we return to the breath. We realize that now we are practicing meditation, so it is not the time to think about those things but to simply pay attention to our breathing. We refocus our attention and say to ourselves, "Now I am placing my mind on the breath."

Beginning to meditate is like learning how to ride a horse: we have to learn to balance. We're learning to balance working with the breath, sitting up straight, and recognizing, acknowledging, and releasing thoughts. We feel like we should be able to do this right away, but meditation is relatively subtle, and getting it all coordinated takes some time. As we're learning to peacefully abide, we'll be falling down, getting up, falling down, getting up. It's important to be gentle and allow a bit of a grace period. We'll tend to hold our mind too tight. We're sitting there, a thought arises, and we think, "Oh! Thoughts are bad." We become irritated trying to deal with the thought, so we over-react and squash it. Yet at this stage a certain amount of thinking is inevitable.

Eventually we begin to realize that the breath itself is soothing. We enjoy the breath. It's not some sort of nasty reminder to work harder. We're simply breathing in and out. It's as if we're discovering for the first time that we are breathing human beings. Then we might go through a period of meditation where we realize, "My goodness, my heart has to beat and my blood has to flow in order for me to stay alive!" We're experiencing our physical body. We're developing the ability to check in with that very basic quality of who we are. We might even experience a level of fear when we see how tenuous it all is.

We need precision to apply the technique and bring our minds back to the breath. It's said that great medi-tators become so centered that they can feel their blood flow. They can actually sense the atomic level of their cellular structure. We need gentleness to keep the process neutral and light-handed. We don't need to analyze or judge a thought when it arises—or judge ourselves for having it. The contents of the thought, whether it's about the football game or our deepest, darkest secret, are neither good nor bad. A thought is just a thought. Chastising ourselves for thinking is also just a thought. So the instruction is to see the thought as a distraction and come back to the breath. This kind of gentleness makes for a healthy meditation practice.

One of the main obstacles to thoroughly enjoying meditation is aches and pains. Our knees throb, our back aches, our shoulders feel tight. The possibility of pain is enough of a deterrent to keep some people from practicing in the first place. I often encounter people who assume that the meditation posture is supposed to be painful. That's unfortunate, because it is meant to feel good. Bodily pain is not a mandatory aspect of meditation. Peaceful abiding is not restricted to our emotional state; meditation relaxes our whole being, which of course includes the body.

Since we may not be accustomed to sitting still for long periods of time without being held up by chairs or pillows, however, we have to be gentle with ourselves. There is a process of getting used to the posture. Westerners often find the idea of sitting on cushions daunting, because we're not used to sitting on the floor. In Tibet and other Asian countries, however, people aren't comfortable sitting in chairs. Halfway through a banquet once, I noticed that Shibata Sensei, my Japanese archery teacher, had given up sitting Western style, drawing his legs into a cross-legged position on his chair. Whether we sit in a chair or on a cushion, the important point is to realize that bodily pain can and should be soothed as we practice. In order to make the journey of meditation, we have to include our body in our practice and allow it to loosen up as the mind relaxes.

Once we've settled into our posture, we make a clear and precise beginning to our practice. It's not necessary to do this with a gong or a bell, the way Buddhists traditionally do; you can just say to yourself something like, "Now I will begin to work with my mind and develop peaceful abiding."

You can start by sitting for ten minutes once a day. If you want to make your session longer, expand it to twenty minutes. If you want to sit more than once, try sandwiching your day between one session in the morning and one in the evening. If you can't practice every day, choose three or four days a week for practice and stay with this schedule. If you're temporarily busier than usual—working on a big project or taking exams, for example—adjust your sitting schedule accordingly and stick with it. Consistency is important. (See Appendix A, "Preparing to Practice," for additional information.)

At the end of your session try not to just jump up and rush back into your daily activities. Enjoy the space that has been created by your meditation, and arise. Perhaps you'll feel a little more fresh, clear, and peaceful than before you started. In daily life, you don't have to carry over any particular technique. Don't eat, drink, or walk like a zombie. You can just relax, and perhaps continue to allow your understanding to deepen. With a mind less busy with thoughts and chatter, you've created helpful space within yourself to carry forward into your day. You'll find it easier to be present both in terms of perceiving what's happening around you and also in communicating more clearly with others. It'll be easier to see thoughts and emotions for the distractions that they are.

The instruction is really pretty simple: when you lose your mind, come back. When the horse runs away with you, bring it back to the trail. Be playful in this. Experiment with tuning in to your sense perceptions, for example, to bring the horse under control. Or practice straightening your posture when you see that your mind has gone wild. Practice meeting the eyes of the person you're with and really listening to what they're saying instead of prefabricating your response as they speak. Use the mindfulness and awareness that you developed on the cushion to stay in the saddle of your life. Then see if you can appreciate these fruits of practice without expectation or attachment.

As meditation becomes part of your life, you might encounter obstacles and questions. It's helpful to have the support of more experienced practitioners who have come face-to-face with similar issues. A meditation instructor can give you tips on aspects of practice that you find difficult. Talking about your experiences with someone else and being part of a community of fellow meditators can be a tremendous support. In the back of this book is a list of resources that might help you in locating a meditation instructor.

Five

Mindfulness and
Awareness

The more consistency with which we practice bringing our mind back to the breath, the more we know that basic stability will be there when we sit down to meditate. How are we going to hold the mind to the breath? Just by taking our seat, we've got the wild horse saddled. Our tools in training it are mindfulness, *trenpa,* and awareness, *sheshin,* "presently knowing." The power of mindfulness is that we can just bring our mind back to the breath; the power of awareness is that we know when to do it. Awareness knows when the horse has bolted, and tells mindfulness to bring it back.

Bringing our minds back to the breath sounds simple, but when we start to practice it, we discover that it's quite the opposite. We're so thoroughly trained in following our thoughts that our mindfulness is weak.

Our awareness isn't too strong, either. At the beginning, it's hard for us to see where we are and what we're doing.

The good news is that mindfulness and awareness are intrinsic aspects of the mind—not something foreign that we're trying to bring in. Mindfulness is what we use to hold our minds to any object—the breath, a rock, or a banana—and awareness is the intelligence that tells us what we're doing. Awareness is what tells us that the phone is ringing. When we answer the telephone, it's mindfulness that holds us to the voice at the other end long enough to know that our mother is calling. So in meditating properly, we're strengthening aspects of our mind that are already there. It's like working out. In developing mindfulness and awareness, the mind begins to feel its strength and its ability to simply be present. We begin to get a glimpse of the mind's natural stability.

When I first started weight training, I could lift only a little bit. But with every repetition, I was building my strength. I didn't become strong from lifting one massive weight at once, but from doing repetitions consistently and regularly and building strength over time. This is exactly how we strengthen mindfulness and awareness—through consistent and regular practice.

As we begin to meditate, what we experience most is the movement of the wild-horse mind. We're following the breath and—whoa!—the horse has gone off the trail and we're lost in the bushes, about to go over a cliff. That ability to notice where we are is awareness. Like a spy on the lookout for trouble, it alerts mindfulness to come and do its job. Sitting tall in the saddle with the reins firmly in hand, we bring the horse back to the trail. In sync with the horse for a moment, we feel tremendous energy and clarity. This is a powerful experience. For a moment our mind can relax and expand out.

Then whoa!—the stallion's caught the scent of a mare. He's been galloping up a hill for some distance before awareness kicks in and tells us that we're no longer on the trail. Our mind has drifted from the breath. We're thinking about the best way to make a salad, or carefully reviewing the last movie we saw. If we let ourselves sit there and think, we are ingraining discursiveness. How do we bring ourselves back to the breath? Time to apply mindfulness. Meditation is proactive.

Mindfulness has three qualities: familiarity, remembering, and nondistraction. Developing these three qualities is how we learn to ride our wild-horse mind. The breath is a mechanism we use to practice centering our mind in the present moment. We begin by using it to become familiar with the mind's natural stability.

At first we're not sure what the breath is, and sometimes we're not able to recognize the present moment, either. Distractions keep pulling us away. After some practice we're able to recognize a thought, let it go, come back, and be present. Sometimes we feel that there is nothing to come back to, so we don't stay around for long. We say, "Nothing interesting here, might as well go back to Tasmania"—or wherever we thought we were before. If we don't become familiar with the inherent stability of the mind, there won't ever be anything interesting about coming back to the present moment. We'll just be holding on by our fingernails because we think we have to. We know that acknowledging, recognizing, and releasing thoughts reduces discursiveness, but we also need positive reasons for coming back to the breath.

This is the virtue of familiarity. Once we relax and get into the movement and rhythm of the breath, the present moment and the breath become very familiar. Our distractions and discursiveness are no longer quite so seductive. By training our horse consistently, we become intimate with how it feels to be peacefully riding the trail. We'd rather return to the present moment than chase a thought, because we're becoming familiar with the stability of our mind and we enjoy it. It's relaxing and comfortable to rest there, like going to our room to be alone when the house is full of people.

The second aspect of mindfulness is remembering. Remembering has an unstudied quality, like not forgetting our own face. It means we're so steady in our mindfulness that we always know what we're doing in the present moment; we're always remembering to hold our mind to the breath. If we're caught up in thought, we're forgetting that we're meditating. When we're replaying last night's hockey game in our head, we've lost our mindfulness. Remembering is like being in love. Wherever you go, your lover is always in the continuum of your mind. You're always conscious of who your lover is, where your lover is, and what your lover might be doing.

In beginning meditation we experience the movement of the wild mind. As we develop mindfulness, becoming familiar with the breath and remembering to return, we finally settle into this continuous state of not forgetting. It takes regular practice. Before, the mind was scattered. As it stabilizes, its natural aspects arise. It has more energy to be where it is—which is mindfulness—and to know what it's doing—which is awareness. The stability provides a continuum that becomes a foundation for building strength.

We see this strength in the third aspect of mindfulness, which is nondistraction. As we develop nondistraction, we place the mind on the breath and it stays. Though it's hard to imagine when we first begin to meditate, if we stick with our practice, our mind's tendency to fly like a horse out of the gate will disappear.

The mind's natural stability and strength will shine through any potential distraction or discursiveness. It sees, it hears, it smells, it thinks, it feels—but it no longer chases wildly after these perceptions. It no longer jumps around. With the mental frequency no longer vibrating with movement, we experience the naturally even and immovable quality of the mind.

When you're training a horse, at first you have to kick it to make it go left. Later all you have to do is make one little finger gesture and the horse immediately does what you want. You're in tune with each other, and there's a sense of complete harmony. Riding doesn't exhaust you—just as meditating won't exhaust you. Once you develop this rapport with the horse, you can let the reins go. The horse will naturally veer away from branches; it will slow down if it's dangerous. With meditation we're developing the same kind of rapport and understanding with our mind. Once we've tamed our mind, it stays in the present moment.

When we have developed the elements of familiarity, remembering, and nondistraction, we can say we are truly mindful. Our mindfulness is mature. We have windhorse—an uplifted feeling of discipline and delight. We're no longer so distracted that when we bring ourselves back to the breath, we have to hold on for dear life. We can see clearly what is. This clarity is able to perceive phenomena very directly. What usually hides it is the discursive activity of thoughts and emotions. As the chatter begins to dissipate, clarity has an opportunity to arise.

This quality of the mind is straightforward and vibrant. There's not a lot of thinking going on, and we perceive very clearly what is happening in our body and in the environment. The mind feels light—and at the same time it is not disturbed, because it is stable. We can experience this same clarity of mind in mundane situations—when the sun comes out after a storm, when we roll in the snow after taking a sauna. In Tibet people say that it's like taking a bath in milk. I went snorkeling recently, and it was a very vivid experience. My body felt light and buoyant, and there was a penetrating clarity to the sunlight shining through the turquoise water on the fish and the coral.

Mindfulness and awareness bring us into such a space, and as we stay there longer, that space gets bigger and bigger. We have the ability to be intimate with the whole environment—our state of mind and the quality of our meditation. Our awareness is so keen that, like a sheriff in the Wild West, it can see trouble brewing before it even hits the horizon. Not only are we able to maintain our seat and keep the horse on the trail, we're also able to extend ourselves panoramically. Before it even arises, we can prevent a thought from destabilizing our mindfulness. This is how we prolong the continuity of peaceful abiding. At this point we can say, "I am mindful of the horse. I am mindful of my meditation. I am mindful of the present moment."

Off the cushion, we're no longer lost in daydreams. We're mindful of our food and it tastes better. We're mindful of sounds—music is more beautiful. We're mindful of the people around us—we appreciate them more. We feel more alive and enthusiastic about life, because there's less buffer between ourselves and what's happening. Our mind is a powerful ally that helps us focus on what we need to do: study, play sports, cook. Everything we do seems more simple, straightforward, and clear.

Total mindfulness means being completely in tune, kind of like the old spiritual jargon of "being one with" something. (However, in Buddhist terms, there is no "one" to be "with.") True mindfulness is no separation between here and there. It's a long way from the beginning of practice, but we can certainly aspire to reach the point where we can say, "I *am* the breath," as opposed to "I know the breath." The sense of separation between our mind and the breath begins to dissolve. At this stage there's nothing to hold on to; we transcend every reference point. The dualistic mind is dissolving. We experience unity with the breath. The less duality we experience, the less we will suffer. Eventually, our dualistic mind exhausts itself. We no longer need an object of meditation. The natural quality of meditation relaxes into boundless, unimpeded freedom and space. The dualistic struggle is over. This is peace.

Before we reach that point of unity with space, the mind has to be strong, stable, and clear. That's why we meditate. Generally speaking, the mind is always outside or inside itself—"inside" in that it's self-obsessed, and "outside" in that it's always leaving. However, by developing mindfulness and awareness, the mind is being drawn back to itself in a positive way: by settling, it becomes an ally. We're completely in tune and harmonious with it, and it's a joy and a relief to be ourselves.

Six

How to Gather
a Scattered Mind

The bewildered mind spends much of its time racing from distraction to distraction, from sound to sight to smell, from feeling to desire to disappointment. It's in a constant state of flirtation. On any given day, our consciousness is fragmented and scattered in all directions. Yet when thunder shakes the sky, we're suddenly sharply focused. For a moment our scattered mind is gathered whole, placed fully on the sound. For a split second we are completely meditating on thunder.

We practice peaceful abiding in order to cultivate that kind of one-pointed attention. It gives us the potential to have stronger, more focused access to whatever we're doing. We settle down to practice in order to draw in the scattered energy of the wild-horse mind. We're bringing the mind to attention. With mindfulness and awareness, we gently and precisely pry our mind away from fantasies, chatter, and subtle whispers of thoughts, placing it wholly here and now upon the breath. We do this because our scattered mind continually seduces us away from our stability, clarity, and strength. So we center ourselves in our mind and place that mind on the breath. We gather it to ground ourselves in a healthy sense of self—wholesome, balanced, confident, pliable.

Gathering the mind is a gradual process. We can imagine the mind's activity as circles of light radiating outward. Peaceful abiding is like taking the dispersed

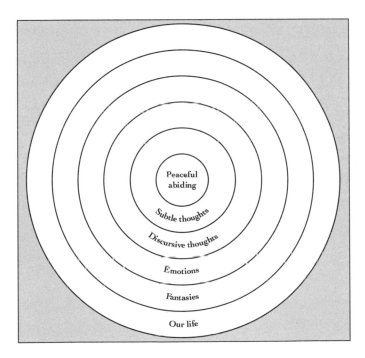

light and gathering it into ourselves. As we gather it closer, it grows brighter. The outermost circle represents our daily life. As we move in toward the center, we work with different levels of thoughts—from the gross to the subtle. The light grows gradually more focused. The point in the middle of the circle represents the fortitude and clarity that underlie the wildness of our scattered mind.

Shamatha practice begins with gathering ourselves at the outermost circle—who we are in our world. Sometimes when I'm instructing children I say, "Sit there and think about who you are. Think about what you like and what you don't like. Think about what it is to be mean and what it is to be kind." We should do this same kind of contemplation before placing our mind on the breath. Perhaps we've never before taken the time to see ourselves so clearly. Making our mind an ally requires self-awareness on every level. So after we sit down and before we begin practicing the technique, we should slow down and reflect on our presence in the world. We need to think for a few minutes about what we like and what we don't like, what we're worried about, and where in our lives we feel a sense of relief. This is how we cultivate self-awareness even at the outer ring of our lives. Having the patience and honesty to be self-aware is the basis of a healthy sense of self. We embody this healthiness in the meditation posture: grounded, balanced, and relaxed. That's what we gather in the outer circle of shamatha.

We take a step into the next circle when we begin to apply the technique, following the breath and acknowledging thoughts as they arise. As new meditators, we'll probably be surprised by how many thoughts we have. When we take our seats and rest our minds on the breath, the sheer volume of thoughts can be overwhelming. This experience is so well documented by the lineage of meditators that it's traditionally described as a waterfall. We're more affected by the volume of water rushing over the falls than by our thoughts' variety or intricacies.

Now we may think, "I wasn't this bewildered before. Meditation has made my state of mind worse. It was supposed to give me peace, liberation, and tranquility, but now I'm more angry and irritated than ever." Either we're right, and meditation does increase mental activity—and all those practitioners over thousands of years, who were some of the most brilliant people ever, were wrong—or maybe we're just recognizing a level of thought and emotion that we had never stopped to notice before. This glimpse of our wild and overheated mind frightens us. Meditation is showing us the nature of the beast. This is why it takes courage to practice peaceful abiding.

At first our practice revolves around just recognizing the individual thoughts in the rush. Finding the breath within the torrent of thoughts might feel impossible. We know it's here somewhere, but when we look for it, we get lost and distracted by the waterfall. This stage is really important, worthy of appreciation. By recognizing the wildness of our mind, we begin to develop synergy with it. Seeing the torrential rain of thoughts is how we begin to train the horse. We can regard this as a positive experience, even though it may not feel that way. We can't possibly meditate without having first experienced the wildness of our mind.

So we simply recognize those thoughts, and then we recognize them again. We're noticing the movement of our mind. Once we've recognized them, we begin to acknowledge them in passing: "Oh! A thought!" The point is to be quick and neutral. If we look at the thought slowly, deliberately, or judgmentally, we'll only add more thoughts to the process. That won't help. A thought has occurred—it is neither good nor bad. Recognizing and acknowledging brings us back to where we are, sitting on a cushion and trying to place our mind on the breath. We're learning how to cut through the discursiveness.

At every stage, shamatha is a practice of noticing how the mind vibrates—how it creates story, speed, and solidity—and learning how to tune it to the present moment. As beginning practitioners, we're acutely aware of the movement of the mind. To recognize a thought is to see the mind vibrating. To acknowledge that we're thinking slows the movement down. When we recognize the mind's movement, we realize the possibility of peaceful abiding. When the mental frequency is no longer vibrating with movement, we experience the naturally even and immovable quality of the mind, if only for a moment.

In gathering our scattered mind we begin to discover who we really are right now, just by seeing that the web of thoughts we solidified as "me" is actually a series of vibrations. If we don't learn to see through this web, however, our continual dreamlike fabrication of "me" will continue to be our meditation. We could be enveloped in it for our whole life. Believing that thought patterns are a solid self is the source of our bewilderment and suffering. Seeing through this simple misunderstanding is the beginning of enlightenment.

The meditation technique engenders clarity because in recognizing, acknowledging, and releasing thoughts, we realize that the mind's movement isn't "me." We don't have to cling to it as if it were a life raft. We'll still be here even if we let go. Releasing the thoughts and returning to the breath gives us a sense of space and relief. In that instant we are grounded, so to speak, because we can see ourselves as separate from our thoughts and emotions. There's distance between ourselves and our thoughts.

Meditation allows us to relax our grip on "me" because we're able to see the thoughts not so much as our personal identity, but more as the effects of the speed of our mind. We gain perspective. We can see the thoughts come and go. We're not so limited by them. Suddenly everything falls into place. We might have spent our entire life—and many lifetimes over, according to the Buddhist teachings—identifying with the movement of our mind. Now mindfulness and awareness present us with the revolutionary opportunity to observe that movement without being swept into it.

It reminds me of rock climbing. If you hold tight to the rock, your forearms lock up and you can't move. There's a paralyzed quality. But if you make some distance between yourself and the rock by relaxing and leaning back, your muscles become flexible and workable. You can make your way along the rock as well as see where you're going. In the same way, by putting distance between ourselves and our thoughts, our minds become more pliable and we have more clarity about our direction in life.

Once we get the hang of acknowledging thoughts and placing our minds on the breath, we take a step in toward the center of the circle. Here we might meet the full-blown fantasy. A fantasy is a very large thought that has the power to take us far, far away from the present moment. It's like a story that we tell ourselves, a movie that we run, a soap opera that draws us in and puts us in a trance. Because it's potent and absorbing, we'd sometimes rather believe a fantasy than reality. Under its spell, we don't even remember that we're meditating.

I once had a student who was in a three-year cabin retreat. At the end of one year, I went to his cabin to discuss his meditation. He told me about some of his experiences — various insights and images had come up — and he had several questions for me. He went into passionate detail about some of his ideas. He seemed to want me to confirm his experience. I listened and assured him that I found his revelations interesting. Without saying that he was right or wrong, I encouraged him to keep practicing.

A year later I paid him another visit. This time he was calmer, more relaxed. About the experiences he'd shared with me before, he said matter-of-factly, "Oh, I dropped all that. I realized it was just a giant thought. It lasted about a year, and in the past few months I've just seen it for what it was and let it go. It felt like dispersing a cloud." He seemed much more at ease with himself, as if he'd made an important and courageous discovery. And he had: thoughts can last for a long time before we recognize them, but if we keep practicing, we will see them for what they are.

If we're fantasizing about going on a long holiday canoeing on the Amazon River, we can see the foliage and taste what we're going to eat at the next meal, but it may take a very long time to notice what we're doing with our minds. When we begin to meditate, we can consider ourselves well-trained if we're just able to see that we're fantasizing, even if we're caught up for most of a meditation session. Sooner or later we see how fantasy—about food, sex, revenge, who said what to whom, or what we're going to do when we're finished practicing—has the power to take over our mind. We begin to see how fantasy can continually keep us from the present moment, how it steals our ability to focus, to move forward in our training. At the end of the session, we can ask ourselves, "How much of the time was I actually here? How many countries and how many people did I visit?" A great deal of the session will have been about dealing with those wild, very intricate thoughts. We use the technique of holding our mind to the breath to help steady us enough to deal with the wild thoughts. Learning to recognize the fantasy and release ourselves from it is how we build up some kind of strength.

The instruction for working with a fantasy is just like the instruction for working with any other thought. As soon as we notice this kind of distraction taking place, we acknowledge it as "thinking" and kiss it good-bye. We have to say good-bye to that very potent thought that might hold all the anger we've cooked up, or all the sexual energy, or all the insecurity. Still, we acknowledge it and return to the breath if we can.

Sometimes it's just asking too much of ourselves to be that precise. Holding the mind too tightly can be harmful. When our control is too tight, the mind will bolt at the earliest opportunity. Fantasy takes us so far away—having a romantic vacation in Tahiti, fighting with our mother in another state—that we aren't even aware of our body, not to mention the breath. Suddenly dropping a very big thought for the immediacy of the breath can be too harsh. In working with large thoughts, upsizing the object of our meditation offers a more gentle approach. We can change the size of the pasture for the horse.

One way to work with large thoughts is simply to bring yourself back to the room you're sitting in. Try to remain present in the room and let the environment ground you until you feel yourself in your body. Then reconnect with the breathing. If there are small thoughts coming up, we might appreciate them, "Before, I was thinking about being at the North Pole. Now I'm wondering what's for dinner. That's an improvement." And it is: at least we're here. If we have a couple of smaller thoughts, that's not a problem. We are at least *somewhat* here. Coming back in stages and gradually re-engaging the breath is one of the most effective ways to work with fantasies.

Fantasies play a large supporting role in maintaining the "have a nice day" approach. They feed on hope and fear, which creates worry. We don't need to spend our meditation worrying. Worrying and anxiety lead to stress, and stress causes suffering. The suffering created by hope and fear routinely clouds our perception of what is happening in the present moment. We're busy spinning out best- and worst-case scenarios, rather than relaxing where we are.

Our root fantasy is that "I" am real and that there's a way to make "me" happy. The reason we meditate is to let that fantasy unravel. After a while, we notice that much of what we took to be real and permanent about ourselves isn't so solid—it's a string of thoughts we hold together with tremendous effort. We've built an identity out of a thin web of concepts. It can be as simple as thinking that we'll be happy if we just get what we want.

As we venture into the next circle of shamatha, we encounter strong emotions. Even in our most tranquil, open-minded state, it is hard to work with emotions. So first we slow down, breathe, and stabilize our mind. Then we can take one of two approaches. The first one depends on our ability to stick with the technique. If we've developed our practice to the point where we can just breathe and let a strong emotion go, that's what we should do. Relying on our stable mind, we can let the power of our meditation bring us back to the breath, which gives us space. Then the emotion begins to lose its grip.

The other approach is to dismantle the emotion by contemplating it. Dismantling is grounded in knowing that no matter how solid the emotion feels, it's fabricated. Everything in the world is made of parts, and emotion is no different. The most painful, powerful aspect of negative emotions is that they seem complete and whole. A thought builds into a crescendo called emotion, which we then embody. The tight ball of hatred, desire, or jealousy feels so solid that we actually feel it in our body as a lump in our throat, a rising wave of heat, an aching heart. When we're caught up in negativity, it's hard to imagine penetrating it, cracking its shell. If we're caught in hatred, for example, it possesses us totally—body, speech, and mind. Even if we don't act it out by shouting at someone or slamming a door, we let it burn like a wildfire in our mind, stoking it with thoughts of aggression, the desire to do harm.

Let's say we're flying in an airplane. In one moment the flight attendant is serving us food and drink, and in the next the airplane makes a sudden drop. One minute we feel safe, then fear is all there is. Even though the pilot quickly regains control of the plane, it takes us a long time to regain control of our mind. Even when we're safely on the ground, the fear is so solid that we feel nervous about flying again.

Especially as we develop stability and balance, we begin to see how our mind forms itself into various emotions.

An emotion that feels as big as a house can be dismantled brick by brick. In dismantling, we use the emotion as the object of meditation. Emotion is a response to something or somebody. It isn't premeditated or logical in any way. The way dismantling works is that we engage the missing element: reason. We begin investigating the feeling: "Why am I jealous? What has made me feel this way?" For a moment we rest our mind on these questions instead of the breath. The more reason we have, the more effective our ability to dismantle will be. In contemplating the reasons that our negative emotions have come together—and how they create pain, suffering, and anxiety—we can begin to take them apart. With reason we see the source of the emotion: what somebody said to us, the disappointment of an expectation we were holding.

Maybe the reason isn't a person, but an object—a chair or a car or a piece of clothing or food is behind our desire or hatred or jealousy. When we contemplate the emotion, we begin to see that the person or object is not the reason for what we feel. *We're* the reason. The emotion is a creation of our mind. We've turned a thought into a seemingly solid entity and held on to it.

In every emotional situation, there's a subject, an object, and an action. For example, riding in a car in India is a frustrating experience. The roads are barely wide enough for one car, and they're very bumpy. When you're stuck behind a slow truck that's spewing diesel smoke—as it seems they all do—there's every reason to want to pass, but it's rarely possible. You become obsessed with the road, the truck, and your desire, and after a while all you can think about is how angry you are. When you finally pass, you see that the truck driver is just a poor man trying to eke out a living. Your anger lightens immediately.

In this situation, the subject is "me," the object is the truck, and the action is being stuck behind it. The pain of the situation is also the object. You're angry at the truck for being where it is, and at yourself for being where you are. You're also angry at being stuck in traffic, and you're angry at being angry. These are the components of this emotion.

As we think about these components, the anger falls apart. The thought draws us closer to the anger, which is important: keeping our distance from emotion has a solidifying effect. By contemplating it, we begin to weaken its power to hold us captive, which creates space. The coolness of reason—looking at the emotion, questioning where it came from, seeking the source, investigating the object—dissipates the heat of the emotion. We begin to wonder why we invest so much energy in this feeling that we've created with our own mind. The bottom line is that everything comes together, and everything falls apart. Slowly we regain perspective, calm, composure, and dignity. We see that there is no anger, no desire, no attachment. Our mind feels lighter, and we can once again place it on the breath.

Sometimes neither letting go nor dismantling works. We're too traumatized to use intelligence or logic, or to recognize and release. We're totally possessed, and contemplating the emotion only inflames it further. We're too close to the action. It's too soon to investigate the scene of the accident. In this case we need to calm down and relax. The best thing might be to get involved in a soothing activity: go for a walk, take a shower, read a book, talk to a friend, watch a movie. When we're calmer, we can come back to the cushion. Knowing when we can meditate is honest meditation.

In the next circle of shamatha we meet discursive thoughts or wildness. These thoughts are distracting, but not nearly as powerful or disruptive as fantasies or strong emotions. Discursiveness is the chatter that constantly clutters our minds, the routine mental buzz. It's made of random, nonassociated thoughts as opposed to fully drawn-out story lines. Even though it's more permeable than fantasy or strong emotion, this ordinary discursiveness is adept at keeping us trapped in "me." It's like a low-level hum that obscures our natural clarity. As we meditate, we can bounce back and forth in our mind about what's going on at school or work, conversations we had—or would like to have—plans for the rest of the day, and basically still be aware that we're meditating. Occasionally we surface from these excursions into the past and future by returning to the breath, but then the movement of our mind invites us to wander off again.

Discursiveness feels like flipping through television channels: an old movie here, sports there, a soap opera over there, and now the news. We might experience it as the nagging desire to scratch our nose, or as wondering how many minutes before our session's over. Discursiveness has the quality of high vibration, which has a peculiarly deadening effect. At the end of twenty minutes of meditation it can leave you thinking, "What was *that*?"

In working with discursiveness, we might be tempted to be loose in our control. However, it's essential to repeatedly place our mind on the breath. Recognize the thought, acknowledge it, let it dissolve, and return to the breath. This breaks up the river of discursiveness. Don't think about what kind of thought you're having—just see it for what it is, and place your mind elsewhere. Experiencing the mind's movement at this level is much of our training in shamatha. Working steadily with wild chatter in meditation makes maintaining mindfulness much easier to do during daily life.

In working with discursiveness, our practice becomes very precise. This precision takes us to the innermost circle of peaceful abiding, where we become aware of very subtle thoughts arising in our stillness. It's like standing next to an iced-over mountain stream; we hear water popping up in tiny bubbles. The thoughts come through like whispers. In our steady mindfulness of the breath, a little voice breaks through, "Am I doing this right? I feel chilly." Even though the surface is still, there is an ongoing flow of water gurgling beneath. We call these "subtle thoughts."

As long as we stay focused on the breath, we can just let these thoughts arise and fall. Subtle thoughts will naturally dissolve. Indulging these subtle movements by giving them any attention at all tends to strengthen them and actually create disturbance in our mind. At some point, of course, we will have to deal with them. But in the early stages of shamatha, we build another kind of strength by relaxing into the breathing. This allows the natural stillness of the mind to develop. Continually placing our mind on the breath decreases the movement of thoughts, which further calms the mind. Experiencing the stability and joy of our mind becomes much more appealing than listening to our mental chatter. We see that the experience of peaceful abiding is simply a gradual reduction of thoughts. At the center of the circles, we meet our mind abiding in basic goodness.

Seven

The Virtues of Boredom

In the Shambhala community, we have as part of our curriculum a one-month program in which participants practice peaceful abiding all day, with walking-meditation breaks and Shambhala yoga. They take their meals in the Japanese monastic style called *oryoki*. This means being silent and meditating for about twelve hours a day. All sorts of funny and interesting things happen over the course of a month, both inside the mind and within the community — everything from fantasies about a person sitting across the room to meditation-hall giggle fits. These waves of energy are reflections of people struggling with boredom.

The fear of boredom often keeps people from meditation. I hear it all the time, "You mean I'm just supposed to sit there doing nothing? I'll be bored to death!" We're afraid there will be nothing to entertain us, nothing to hold our interest. In meditation, we're isolating ourselves. First we isolate the body in a very quiet place with as little external stimulation as possible. We place it on a cushion in a very simple posture. Then we isolate our mind. We place it upon the breath and practice keeping it there. Eventually we reduce the number of thoughts. If we're able to slow down and abide in our internal space, we'll begin to appreciate the lack of stimulation in meditation compared to the chaos of normal life. But we will be bored at times, because we won't always want to be where we are.

Sometimes boredom helps us enjoy the simplicity of meditation. At other times boredom is a threat to our practice, a no-man's-land where we're unable to fully experience peaceful abiding. Being bored may even incite us to walk away from the cushion.

There are several kinds of boredom. One kind of boredom has an undercurrent of anxiety. We're not altogether comfortable with ourselves. When we sit down to meditate, we suddenly have no external amusement. Our senses are habituated to speed and stimulation. Without being stimulated, we find no way to satisfy ourselves. We feel stir crazy, like a child with nothing to do. The agitation wants to reach for something to fill the space. If we were waiting at the airport or the doctor's office, we'd reach for a magazine, the cell phone, or a computer game. But in meditation there's nothing to reach for. We try to cope by making our own entertainment. Instead of following the breath, we'll amuse ourselves with a little sound or the movements of an insect. Watching others meditate in front of us can seem as interesting as a full-length feature film.

Another kind of boredom is rooted in fear. We're afraid of being left alone with ourselves because we're not able to relax with our mind. It's like sitting next to an acquaintance at a dinner party, having heard that his wife has just left him and that no one's supposed to know. We feel awkward and uncomfortable. We're wary of opening a conversation because we're afraid of where it might lead. Just so, in meditation we're fearful because we're not accustomed to resting with no activity. It's too quiet. We're not sure we want to know what will happen if we totally let go into the space. We want to maintain our comfort zone. We're unable to go deeper with ourselves, and there's nothing else to do. The result is fearful boredom. This fear comes from not being able to imagine the mind at peace.

These first two kinds of boredom contain a slight quality of aggression that keeps us from practicing properly. We want things to be different from how they are. We've been sitting there in meditation waiting for something to happen or not to happen, and we feel angry and frustrated at our predicament. We can take another approach by observing the boredom and letting ourselves taste it completely. This is a good way to gauge our progress. Look how far we've come: in the beginning we couldn't sit still, we didn't like our water-fall of thoughts, and we could barely fight the constant urge to get up and do something else. We thought of washing the dishes, making lists of what we needed to do at work, and of returning phone calls. Our mind was so speedy that our body wanted to get off the cushion to relieve the pressure. Now things move a little more slowly, and the impulses to move don't seem as strong. We're faced with the boring quality of meditation and it makes us want to quit. If we don't give in to this impulse, we'll begin to reap the benefits of boredom.

We start to do this when we settle in to our bore-dom. We're stuck on the cushion where nothing is going to happen, and we know it, so we begin to just settle in. We may sink into ourselves and become some-what glazed over. The world feels distant and fuzzy. Perhaps we don't quite embrace our practice, but we are able to relax enough to experience the dullness without grasping at amusement or pushing away the space. We've begun to accept boredom as part of the landscape of peaceful abiding. That's progress.

What are we bored with when we meditate? It's not peaceful abiding, even though meditation may be the trigger. What we're really bored with is our repetitive thought patterns. Even though they've become predictable and transparent to us, somehow they keep arising. We see how we get hooked into chasing fantasies and schemes that have as much substance as last night's dream. We discover that the thought, "What's for lunch?" never tastes anything like the meal. We see that philosophizing about practice can't hold a candle to being grounded in the present moment. After a while our boredom takes on a seasoned quality. It's no longer needy; it's spacious, comfortable, and soothing. My father called this "cool boredom." This is a breakthrough. We've discovered that meditation isn't going to fulfill our need for entertainment or fortify our comfort zone. In order to make that discovery, we need to be thoroughly bored.

Being fully bored with our wild mind and continuing to apply the technique represents the point at which we personally commit to the practice of peaceful abiding. We see the tricks we play on ourselves with thoughts, emotions, and concepts. All of it is boredom — our need for entertainment, our fear of our own aloneness, any desire we have to gain something from meditation. This boredom is not a problem. It inspires us because we don't feel trapped on the cushion anymore; we see how our mind works and we feel enthusiastic about developing an alliance with it. We can relax. Seeing the process of mind clearly is what strengthens our commitment to practice. A certain joy develops because we're no longer resisting any part of the landscape.

I remember once participating in a ritual that lasted several weeks with His Holiness Dilgo Khyentse Rinpoche. We were sitting in a very hot meditation hall, listening to him read from a text for about eleven hours a day. This is called "oral transmission," and it's an important ceremony. We sat cross-legged on mats while volume after volume was read aloud in such rapid-fire Tibetan that it was nearly impossible to follow. People fidgeted and whispered, and some of the young monks in the back got into rice-throwing wars. We didn't know how long it would take to read through this text, but each day we hoped the next day would be the last.

Over the course of about two weeks we watched the stack of texts gradually grow smaller until finally only one volume remained. We were sure that there would only be one more day of the oral transmission, and we were ecstatic. It was unbearably hot and humid, and we hadn't had a day off to rest or get to the store or even wash our clothes. We were all so exhausted by the end of each day that we'd just fall into bed.

On the last day, we awaited the closing announcements. We were in for a surprise. Rinpoche told us that we were very fortunate because the final missing volumes of the text had been found. The ceremonies and the reading went on for another week or so, and there was nothing left to do but relax and enjoy being there.

Sometimes we just can't settle in. If boredom starts taking its toll with the result that we want to avoid meditating, we need to do something to counter that pattern. We can start by experimenting with our practice. We can focus on different aspects of the practice at different times. One day we can highlight awareness of the posture. We follow the breath and recognize thoughts, but we pay extra attention to the body. At another time we can become intimate with the process of breathing. In the next session we can sharpen our ability to spot thoughts or to cut through a chain of discursiveness that's taken us on vacation to the Himalayas. Then we might focus on the recognizing process—on spotting the tail end of a thought, for example. By emphasizing different components of the technique, we are strengthening mindfulness and awareness. Of course, another aspect of this mobility in practice is knowing when to return to the simple instructions and put precise focus on the breath.

Everyone has days when practice is difficult and boring. It can help to be aware of our state of mind before taking our seat. When we enter a session of meditation and can sense that we're totally distracted, for example, we might try sitting down on the cushion and thinking away. We can think about whatever difficulty we're facing and let the thoughts and fantasies play out. But we do it with awareness. Then after ten minutes of thinking, we place our mind on the breath.

Sometimes reason and antidotes seem to have no effect. During these periods we need to dig deep and find the strength to continue, or examine our life to see if the pain or the intensity we experience in meditation stems from difficulties elsewhere. Shamatha is not an endurance test, nor will it suddenly solve all our problems. But it does help us see how our problems arise, because it trains us in recognizing thoughts and emotions. It also trains us in letting them pass without acting on them.

Even when we're bored, we can work with our minds. This helps us cope in daily life. Because practice has enlarged our perspective beyond identifying with our thoughts and opinions, we're less likely to act from a tight, self-protected space. We have more patience, more tolerance. We're more able to put ourselves in someone else's shoes. In this way, meditation matures us.

Eight

Laziness

About twenty years ago, my father and I visited the samurai lineage master Shibata Sensei, my Japanese archery (*kyudo*) teacher. Shibata Sensei is the Imperial Bow Maker to the emperors of Japan. His responsibilities include performing a ritualized ceremony at a famous shrine where his family has been making offerings for generations. The year I was visiting, Sensei's son, heir to the family lineage, was going to shoot the ceremonial arrow before the shrine. But he had badly cut his finger while making a bow just days before the ceremony, and was unable to shoot.

At about five A.M. on the ceremonial day I was awakened and told that I was to perform the ceremony as a representative of the Shambhala Buddhist lineage and Sensei's family. I thought they were joking. While I had been practicing archery for many years, I had no idea how to perform the elaborately choreographed bows and gestures in this particular ceremony.

By the time I was ready to go, Sensei had already headed over to the shrine. I couldn't believe this was happening. I was going to be the first non-Shibata to make an offering at this shrine, and I had no idea what I was doing. When I arrived, people started dressing me in official robes. It was like being dressed for a play without knowing my lines. There were hundreds of dignitaries, spectators, and photographers out there waiting to begin. I tried to ask for some instructions, but no one could explain the whole thing in a hurry. I decided just to do my best.

As it turned out, Sensei had organized things so that he would be my assistant. He said that if I made the wrong move, he would be there to whisper directions to me—but he barely knew any English. So we went through the ceremony with him whispering "Left, bow, right, bow . . . move fan, bow," and I shot the ritual arrow. In the end it all worked out, and I couldn't believe that I had done it. Sensei was so happy that afterward he took me out to lunch at his favorite noodle shop.

The power of being put on the spot like this was that it took me beyond the limits of what I thought I could do. We need this same kind of challenge in our practice, because our natural state lies beyond the reach of what we conceptually know. The reason we work so hard to gather our minds is in effect so we can relax. By releasing the web of beliefs and concepts that holds our sense of self solid, we're softening the ground of basic goodness so that love and compassion can break through. If we meditate long enough, we'll discover no shortage of obstacles to this process.

Obstacles are habitual patterns that keep our minds small, fixed, and solid. If we want our minds to be soft and pliable, we will need to know how to work with them. There are outer obstacles like laziness—common laziness, disheartenment, and speedy busyness. These have the power to keep us from ever reaching the cushion. Then, once we make it to our seat, there are inner obstacles such as forgetting the instructions, elation, and laxity.

Like weeding a garden, dealing with obstacles is an ongoing aspect of meditation. Working with these challenges on the cushion is another way we build confidence and courage to go further. We can be grateful for obstacles, because they push us forward in our practice. After a while it is even possible to feel a spark of delight when we see an obstacle coming up, because we know it's an opportunity to keep sharpening our minds. The more obstacles we face, the more confidence we feel to deal with them.

One of the most challenging obstacles for a beginning meditator is laziness. Laziness can be an obstacle even before we reach our seat, because it can keep us from ever getting there. The Tibetan word for laziness is *lelo*, which is pronounced "lay low." In any culture, laziness means lying as low as possible. Laziness has a draining quality, as if we're low in life force. Sometimes it's hard to see it because it feels like who we are. It encroaches on our most intimate ground. It manifests as an allegiance to comfort. We may get plenty of sleep, but we're completely uninspired. We'd rather lie around on a couch watching television, or read a magazine and pass out on the floor.

I have a friend who's particularly susceptible to attacks of basic laziness. For example, one day when we were relaxing together, he decided to take a rest on the couch. He poured himself a drink, placed it on the coffee table, and then lay down on the sofa. After a few minutes of lying there, he realized he'd placed his glass on the far side of the table, out of reach. Instead of sitting up and picking up his glass, he found a clothes hanger that was wedged between the cushions and hooked the leg of the coffee table with it to drag the table closer. Predictably, the drink fell off the table. We often expend much more energy being lazy than it would take to deal with our life straightforwardly.

We have to understand that from a meditative point of view, laziness is a particular way of holding the mind. The mind has withdrawn into itself. In its more extreme versions—when we are *really* lazy—the whole world seems very distant. It seems impossible to do anything. We feel like a snake crawling along the ground. Everything else is in the treetops, up high and far away. If someone says, "Why don't you *do* something?" we feel irritated and upset. We can't deal. We're all dug in, like an animal in a hole. We're not interested in exterior things. Our mind is encapsulated in itself.

If we're feeling lazy, even if we somehow make it to our seat, we'll spend the session avoiding the basic technique. We don't even have the energy to sit up straight. We can't practice properly. We think, "I just don't want to do it. I don't have time." Worse yet, "I don't really need to do it." Whatever we're telling ourselves, at the root of laziness lies attachment. We're attached to the comfort of familiar fantasies and discursive thoughts; we prefer them to the wakeful quality of following the instructions with precision.

This pattern is an obstacle to meditation. If we don't see it, we can get stuck in laziness for a long time—even years. It's especially insidious because we lull ourselves into believing that a certain amount of thinking is okay. If we have a major thought or daydream, we usually recognize it and acknowledge it. But one of the symptoms of laziness is that we let a whole middle range of thoughts pass. We feel that it's just too much to meditate for the whole twenty minutes or half an hour, so we'll use fifteen minutes to think about what a great time we had at last night's party, or to plan today's outing. We think, "No one knows what I'm doing with my mind, so I'll use the time to plan. Then I'll meditate for five or ten minutes just to make myself feel better." It's like going into a supermarket just to buy corn on the cob and potato chips and then wandering the aisles to look for other items. When we let ourselves hang out in discursive chatter, we're wandering around snacking in our minds. If we allow ourselves to hang out there for long, our whole meditation will eventually consist of middle-range thoughts that are seemingly not all that harmful.

When my mother moved from India to the United States, she was amazed by the vastness of our supermarkets and intrigued by all the products available. What most surprised her were the aisles of pet food. She was a little shocked at the amount of attention paid to the culinary needs of cats and dogs and the money spent on satisfying them. In India, a dog is fortunate to be given leftover rice. Many a dog in India spends its whole life prowling for food.

If we have a tendency to prowl through our minds in meditation, we should tell ourselves before sitting down that we're not going to be seduced by our discursiveness. When we find ourselves doing it, we need to acknowledge that we're doing something besides meditating, and that it isn't benefiting our meditation. We have to recognize, acknowledge, and release these middle-range thoughts. Unless it's a thought like, "I smell smoke. Is the house on fire?" we should return our mind to the breath. The thoughts, the brilliant ideas, and the decisions to be made will still be around when we've finished meditating.

Laziness also manifests as busyness. Speediness is laziness when we use it as a way to avoid working with our minds. When we first begin to meditate, we're enthusiastic about rearranging our priorities around a daily practice. What we don't count on is the force of habit. Staying busy can be a way to avoid meditation. All of a sudden, right before we mean to meditate, suddenly we need to tend to little tasks—watering plants, brushing our teeth, checking our e-mail. Not only that, we need to do these tasks right now. This is speedy laziness—better known as procrastination. This force can become especially compelling when shamatha practice provides a glimpse of how naturally open and joyous our minds truly are. Resisting our own openness by spinning the stories that keep us in the comfort zone of "me" is a very old and well-established habitual pattern. Procrastination is one way of choosing to abide in distraction rather than to relax into the peace of our mind.

Another way we procrastinate is by using seemingly worthy activities to avoid meditating. Perhaps we're even helping animals or other people. Even though these activities are beneficial to others, if we want to meditate and we're using them as an excuse not to, we need to look at it clearly by asking, "Is my lifestyle supporting my practice? Are my activities beneficial in terms of meditation?"

Obviously, meditation can sometimes be difficult. We may want to run away from practice, run from the cushion, even run from the word "meditation." We can run as far as we like, but what we'll discover is that there is no better environment than meditation in which to build the stability, clarity, and strength of our mind. At the same time, the difficulty of making it to the cushion, the difficulty of staying with the technique, the difficulty of abandoning discursiveness, isn't going to disappear. In procrastinating, we're avoiding the one thing that really is going to make a difference in our lives. Meditation stabilizes us in our inherent power as humans. It introduces the possibility of living our lives in a continually conscious, confident, and balanced state of mind.

Another kind of laziness is disheartenment. We feel discouraged, deflated, or outnumbered by the obstacles that arise in our practice. We take them personally. Our belief in the solidity of the obstacles grows, and our belief in our ability to practice shrinks. We say, "How can I possibly develop an ongoing meditation practice?" If we are already meditating, we say, "How can I possibly finish this session?" Before we know it, we feel hopeless about meditating.

When my father passed away in 1987, His Holiness Dilgo Khyentse Rinpoche led the traditional funeral rites. Afterward he recommended that we build a 108-foot tall stupa in the Rocky Mountains to com-memorate my father's years of work in introducing Buddhism to North America and teaching meditation to Westerners. A stupa is a traditional sacred structure representing the enlightened mind of the Buddha. Building one involves following many intricate and precise traditional specifications. We felt slightly over-whelmed by the complexity of the project, the first of its magnitude in North America. We started building it in 1988, continuing to work on it every summer.

Each year we had to gather all kinds of resources. Hundreds of hands-on volunteers were involved. The people closest to the project had to dig deep into their own resources, spending cold winters and hot summers in the Rockies over a thirteen-year period. In a sense we learned how to build the stupa as we built it. The engineering, the construction, the finances, and the traditional artwork—all of these elements presented daunting challenges. What spurred us on was our trust that this symbol of enlightenment would be of great benefit to everyone. As the stupa took form, our confidence and energy increased. Watching it rise into space little by little, we overcame our doubt and hesitation. In the summer of 2001 the stupa was complete, and we held a beautiful consecration ceremony attended by thousands of people. We had encountered all kinds of obstacles, but our inspiration was an antidote to all of them.

The teachings on obstacles and antidotes come from a very long lineage of meditators in India and Tibet. We're fortunate that they documented the difficulties so well, because even though the conditions in which we practice might differ greatly from theirs, the obstacles that arise on the path of meditation have never changed. Luckily, the antidotes have also passed the test of time and space.

Laziness is a symptom that we've lost connection with the courage that brought us to the cushion in the first place. We no longer understand why we're meditating. We feel slightly threatened by letting go of the comfort of thought patterns. Meditation goes against the grain of habits we've accumulated for a long, long time. Most of these habits concern the perpetual creation of "me." We're habitually indentured to fabricating projections, scenarios, opinions, and story lines that we use to hold our creation together. With meditation it can feel as if we're falling apart. Old habits can start to look very comforting, because they represent who we think we are. We find ourselves reverting to ingrained patterns in order to strengthen that self-created concept of "me." Meditation is about seeing through the contrived sense of "me" as the enlightened aspects of the mind reveal themselves. We have to let that fabrication dissipate in order to go forward, and it makes us feel uneasy.

What the meditators of old discovered is that the key to success in meditation lies in connecting with a bigger view. They suggest four ways in which we can inspire ourselves—suppleness, trust, aspiration, and effort.

Suppleness

A lazy mind is a mind that has become small and fixated. Meditation doesn't fit in with our habitual patterns, so we resist it. A supple mind has many more possibilities because it is flexible. It doesn't look at the world from the closed system of "me," so it's no longer bound by the constrictions of maintaining its own comfort zone. In Tibetan the word for this kind of mind is *shinjang,* meaning "thoroughly trained." Two qualities of the shinjang mind are pliability and interest. This mind is curious. It doesn't fall into laziness and the other obstacles because it knows how to stay open. That's the point of meditation, isn't it? We want to develop an open, interested, flexible mind. When we have a supple mind, obstacles to our meditation don't occur.

Our minds become more supple as we develop ourselves on the meditation seat. Each time we acknowledge a fantasy or thought, we're softening up our mind by becoming less bound to concepts and emotions. Following the technique fosters curiosity instead of dullness, appreciation instead of disheartenment, and imagination instead of limitation.

In order to overcome laziness, we need to have a relatively open mind from the very beginning. We need to be curious, to have a sense of appreciation and imagination. We need to inspire ourselves. For example, we might not feel like going for a hike, but when a friend shows us a picture of an amazing mountain, its beauty inspires us; it breaks through our laziness. Before, our mind was closed — now there's workability. We're rousing windhorse by stepping out of that sunken state of mind. In the same way, we can overcome laziness by being open and imaginative.

Trust

When we've heard the teachings and also experienced their true meaning—that to practice shamatha is to abide peacefully—a certain faith develops. This isn't blind faith. It's based on our own relationship with meditation. We have faith in a practice that we've experienced ourselves.

We take trust from clarity and confidence. Perhaps a moment of clarity is what inspired us to practice in the first place. We saw a statue of the Buddha, read a book, or even saw a friend meditating, and we had an immediate sense of clarity about wanting to do this. Having tested shamatha through discipline and precise attention, we know that we can trust the technique. We're clear about how it works because we've done it ourselves. We've seen how stiff, wild, and raw our mind is. We've had moments of peacefully abiding. We've seen that our mind doesn't always have to be a nuisance. We've felt the openness of our hearts underneath the hardness of habitual pattern. We're constantly reevaluating and deepening our understanding of meditation, because it goes awry very quickly. This process builds confidence. We can use this trust to remind ourselves of why we should practice even when we don't want to.

Inspiration is an immediate longing, a sudden flash we can use to recharge our batteries. It's like imagining a cold glass of lemonade on a hot summer day. The thought of the ice, the sharp taste, the frosted glass, even the slice of lemon on the edge rouses us out of our sweaty lawn chair and into the kitchen for refreshment.

In the same way, we can use our longing for the freshness of the mind at ease to bring us to the cushion, to bring us to the technique. We remember the cool peaceful place that underlies the oppressive heat of our bewilderment and suffering. We long to be there. We trust the refreshing and joyous aspects of meditation because we've heard about them, we've studied them, and we've experienced them. This is the support we need to move beyond disheartenment and procrastination.

Aspiration

The next antidote is aspiration. Aspiration is trust with a sense of determination. We're determined to discover our own awakeness. We aspire to be like the Buddha, like someone who has mastered their whole being, someone who realizes the profound truth of things as they are. We've seen the volatility of external conditions. We've become dissatisfied with hope and fear as a way of life. Now we aspire to depend on our own stability, clarity, and strength.

This determination is strong enough to overcome any resistance. When we're on the meditation seat and find ourselves wandering into laziness, our aspiration to soften the hardness of our mind is what inspires us to apply the technique and go back to the breath. A flash of wanting our mind to be at ease in its own strength can be enough to dissipate our laziness.

No one told us to see ourselves as real, and we're certainly not alone in this basic misunderstanding. Laziness can be a form of letting blame sink us back into bewilderment and suffering: "This culture just keeps everyone asleep. No one else is meditating. Why should I be different? I think I'll just wait it out for a while." The Buddha says that if we look at it that way, we'll be waiting for a very long time. We may never get around to practicing. We have to accept responsibility for the state of our own mind; it doesn't work to blame others for our confusion or expect them to encourage or confirm us in our practice. We have to look to ourselves as the source of our own confusion—and our own enlightenment.

Meditation is like making a friend who gives us good advice about how to live our life, how to handle our mind, how to see ourselves as intrinsically awake.

It has already begun to untangle our bewilderment. We've seen the power of meditation to restore our sanity, to restore our well-being. Aspiration is a deep desire to go further.

It's as if we're climbing a mountain and we come to a place where we're tired and winded and we think we just can't go any farther. We stop to rest and look back to see how far we've come. We're amazed by how high we are and how far we've climbed. In Tibet, when we reach a place like this, we shout the warrior's cry— "*Ki ki so so, lha gyel lo!*" Essentially this means, "The view is victorious!" The power of the big view gives us the courage to keep going. That's how aspiration overcomes laziness.

Effort

If we think that by simply getting ourselves into the right position, our meditation will take place, we're wrong. Meditation is proactive. We have to be part of the process. That doesn't mean grinding it out. It means the mind must be engaged.

The power of the engaged mind is that it moves toward the act of meditating. That's effort. It's the opposite of laziness, which is holding back. If we don't have mental effort, we're going to drift away. It takes effort to pull ourselves out of laziness and get to our seat. It takes effort to follow the technique correctly. Although shamatha is abiding in peace, it takes effort to stabilize our wild mind in that peace. This energy comes directly from our trust and aspiration. The symbiotic relationship between inspiration and effort makes us eager to engage in meditation.

His Holiness Penor Rinpoche is one of the few genuine meditation teachers still alive today. He is always an inspiration to me, particularly as someone who exerts himself continually for others and who seems to find joy and energy in the effort. This is a true sign of an accomplished meditator.

After he and many thousands of people escaped from Tibet into India, there were few places for monks and nuns to find food and shelter, let alone continue meditation practice. So Penor Rinpoche decided to re-establish his lost monastery in India. He had to clear a jungle and raise money in tiny increments, but he eventually built the monastery with his own hands. Now, it continues to grow and thrive with thousands of people benefiting. Penor Rinpoche still works tirelessly, with many administrative, financial, and educational responsibilities.

Despite his constant exertion, he is unwavering in his energy. He's cheerful—always joking and telling stories. He is completely present for a sick and dying person in one moment, and then in the next for the needs of a young monk in trouble. He doesn't take weekends or breaks, but continually exhibits this joyous effort day after day, filling people with confidence. He once told me that he doesn't worry very much, "Life is more difficult if you worry. It's better to deal with things as they come up."

He is truly an example of someone who applies effort fluidly. Clearly this doesn't mean that he lives a quiet, isolated life. He is constantly busy and faced with obstacles, but he faces them with equanimity, joy, and a strong and stable mind. This is meditation in action. Practicing exertion like this helps us to turn the tide of laziness in our practice and in our daily life and trains us to live with confidence and strength.

Nine

Forgetting the Instructions

The second obstacle is forgetting the instructions. When we first begin to meditate, we're told how to hold our bodies on the cushion and how to hold our mind to the object of meditation. With mindfulness and awareness, we recognize and acknowledge thoughts and return our focus to the breath. That's our basic instruction. As soon as the mind leaves the breath and goes elsewhere, we have encountered the obstacle of forgetting the instruction. This pattern routinely blocks the road of meditation.

When we forget the instructions, what we're holding our mind to is discursiveness. We're on the cushion so wrapped up in thought that we can't remember what we're supposed to be doing. The instruction to stay present seems weak compared to the power of our distractions. Forgetting the instructions can happen suddenly or it can happen gradually, as if we're losing our grip on a heavy object. No matter how hard we try, we can't stay focused on the breath. The technique becomes blurry. Nothing inspirational comes to mind. We can only remember a couple of words: "sit," "breath," "thought," "mind." Apart from that, we can't remember anything. Not only have we forgotten the simple instructions, we might also have forgotten the view—the reason we're meditating.

One reason we forget the instructions is that we're approaching meditation simplemindedly. We think it isn't that complicated—only a point or two to keep in mind. It's possible for simplicity to work, if we're able to follow the instructions. However, with a simple-minded view, our meditation becomes weak. When we're just waiting for thoughts to pop up like clay pigeons so we can shoot them down, we're forgetting our view and our intention. We're forgetting that we're here to cultivate the mind's natural stability, clarity, and strength. This isn't simplicity, it's lack of perspective. All we have is technique; we've forgotten the reasons for following it. We've forgotten that the view of meditation is to be one-pointed and spacious. That's how we begin to purify our habitual patterns and discover our true nature. If we're employing the technique without the view, then all of a sudden, we can't figure out how to do it at all. Out of pride and lack of time, we may even start inventing our own little meditation technique.

When we look at what actually *happens* in meditation, we see that it isn't simple. In fact, the power of practice comes from the details and the depth: the posture, the breath, the placement of our mind, the intention, and the view. If we lose even one of these threads, the fabric of our practice comes unraveled and we forget what we're doing.

The antidote to forgetting the instructions is mindfulness—in particular, remembering. We need to remind ourselves continuously of the details. If you've forgotten what you're doing with your mind, almost inevitably you've also forgotten what you're doing with your body. Start by remembering your posture. Is your spine still upright? Are you relaxed, or are you holding tension in your shoulders and arms? What are you doing with your gaze? Simply checking your posture and starting your meditation over—"Now I'm placing my mind on the breath"—can be the most direct way to invoke the instructions when you've forgotten in the middle of a session.

The reason we practice every day is that it's easy to stray from the view; everything else in our life pulls us in different directions. We can regard forgetting the instructions as an integral part of our practice. Mindfulness as an antidote means to learn it again. We need to keep remembering what meditation is, why we do it, and how. We need to study and contemplate. Without having a clear idea of what we're doing and refreshing it regularly, our meditation will never be successful. When we reread a meaningful book, for example, our take on it is often completely different from the first time. Obviously the words haven't changed; our understanding has deepened.

No matter how easy meditation practice may sound, once we've tried it, we see that it's a challenging thing to do. There's an element of bravery involved every time we take our seat. Letting go of laziness and applying ourselves with mindfulness takes courage. It means that we are willing to leave our habitual patterns behind and move into new territory. Even though the voice of resistance is telling us, "Forget about it. Go do something else," we persevere, because we know there's no other way to make our mind an ally. At a certain point in our meditation, we know exactly what we're doing. We've burned through enough fantasies, thoughts, and scenarios that we no longer believe them. We realize that all the ways we've kept ourselves asleep have led nowhere. Our wisdom is ripening. We quite gladly meditate, because we see that there is no better way to dissipate bewilderment and suffering.

Ten

Not Too Tight,
Not Too Loose

My golf instructor, Norrie, says that most of us are "outgainers," always looking to outer conditions for success instead of creating the proper conditions within. He considers golf a game of cause and effect in which we're both the cause and the effect: We get mad, and no matter how much we want to cast blame elsewhere, it's we who are to blame. His point is that before taking a swing we have to center ourselves — recognize what we're feeling and come to inner balance — if we want to make a good shot. Otherwise we'll be at the mercy of inner volatility as well as the wind blowing across the course. If we're too wound up or too relaxed, our ability to make the shot is compromised. If we've stabilized ourselves first, we'll naturally be able to make our best swing. In order to do this, we need awareness. Awareness is the ability to know what is going on in our mind at present. It's important in meditation as well as in golf.

The point of awareness—and the point of meditation, for that matter—is to know what's happening. We have to be awake. Otherwise we fall into lethargy, which is one step away from sleep. Without awareness, meditation will lead nowhere. In the first stages of peaceful abiding, awareness acts as a spy who watches us meditate, alerting mindfulness to bring us back to the breath when we stray. For a while it might be clumsy and intrusive, because as beginners we need to be watching constantly. But as we practice, awareness continues to develop. The mind becomes more stable, and our ability to know what's happening becomes stronger. Awareness becomes the sheriff who can sense that our mind is about to become distracted and remedy the situation before it even occurs. We don't see the sheriff running around everywhere; we just know he's there. Because we have more confidence, awareness no longer feels intrusive.

Mindfulness and awareness also have roles as antidotes. For instance, when we face the obstacle of forgetting the instructions, the antidote is to trigger the remembering aspect of mindfulness. In the same way, when facing the obstacles of *göpa* and *chingwa,* elation and laxity, we're calling on awareness as the antidote.

As our practice deepens, we see intricate levels of discursiveness: discursiveness within fantasies, discursiveness within emotions, discursiveness within thoughts, and discursiveness within discursiveness. Conversely, the way awareness comes in and looks at our meditation also becomes subtle. In the beginning it was very hard to see how that level of subtlety might develop. But as time goes on, because mindfulness takes less effort, we have greater awareness to oversee our practice.

Encountering an obstacle is a signal that we're holding our mind to some form of distraction. Elation and laxity arise once we have some stability in our practice. They are mid-level roadblocks. It's possible to get a brief taste of elation and laxity in the earlier stages, but because our mind has to be well gathered in order to experience them fully, these obstacles are signs of progress. They indicate that our mindfulness is strong and our mind is stable. The horse is always staying on the trail, and now we must work with its gait. Occasionally it's taking off after something to eat, and sometimes it's stubbornly spacing out. Because it's no longer rearing or bolting, however, we might hardly notice these other behaviors. It's important to work with them, though, because it's how we begin to find the middle ground of the balanced mind—not too tight and not too loose.

In both elation and laxity, we experience the movement of the mind that keeps us from being fully present. In elation, we're holding our mind so tight that it begins to panic, just as a horse does when we're reining it in too hard. In laxity, we're holding our mind so loose that it drifts away.

In elation, we're focused too tightly on the breath. With no warning, our mind protests by suddenly taking off after some enticing little pleasure: a thought of ice cream, pizza, a cup of coffee, a pleasant past event, romance, sunshine—it could be anything. Suddenly we're no longer in charge. The horse is out of the gate. Why pleasure? After stability is established, it's more common for desire than aggression to disturb our meditation. No matter what stage of practice we're in, it always feels better to want something than to feel anger, jealousy, or pride. We eventually arrive at a place where anger and jealousy and pride no longer arise so much, but pleasurable little desires still hook us. And we don't know we're hooked until our mind is gone.

Laxity is the opposite of elation. In Tibetan the word for laxity is *chingwa*—the word that's used when someone's drowning. It means "to sink." The mind sinks into itself. Our relationship to the breath is loose, fuzzy, and distant. We lack freshness and clarity. We blank out. We've lost our taming power. "Too loose" may feel as if we're not thinking, but what's really happened is that we've deadened our mind. We've suppressed the mind's movement. Because thinking is so neurotic, marauding, tedious, and obnoxious, we've decided to boycott it. That's what laxity feels like. We go to the extreme of trying to do nothing, even though that's not possible: the mind is always generating and being generated.

What's happening in that state, when mind nullifies itself? One scenario is that the thoughts and emotions cancel each other out. Another is that we're trying so hard to be mindful, our mind sinks. When we sit down, we just fall asleep. This is connected with boredom. We're frustrated because we're used to constant entertainment, and now the mind can't even produce remotely interesting thoughts. So it's bored — seemingly with meditation, but actually with itself.

The antidote to both elation and laxity is awareness. We have to look at what's going on in our mind. Once awareness has told us that we're too loose or too tight, we have to learn how to adjust. If the obstacle is elation, we might try relaxing the technique, giving it a bit more room. We could give our outbreath more focus than our inbreath so that the mind has more freedom. Or we could lighten our focus on the breath altogether. In that space, the agitation might settle down and we can go forward with a strong and clear meditation. If the obstacle is laxity, we need to tighten up our practice. We can bring more of our mind to the breathing overall. We could focus on the inbreath. We can stabilize our posture. We might try to perk up by removing a layer of clothing, opening a window, or raising our gaze.

Another obstacle is that at times of great stability the mind does not apply the antidote. For example, we might be feeling relaxed, soothed, and content with our meditation, not recognizing that we're in a state of laxity. Everything feels good, we're in a good mood, and we think we've achieved perfection. Since we don't realize we're facing an obstacle, it's hard to apply an antidote. Yet the appropriate antidote in such a situation is to apply the antidote.

Equally subtle is the obstacle of *over*applying the antidote. Once when I was camping in a beautiful mountain meadow, some of my neighbors were playing a radio. Here we were in a quiet and peaceful place, and they thought they could make it better by adding one more thing. This is overapplying the antidote. It's sometimes best just to let our practice be. If we fiddle with it too much, we'll only be stirring up water that has settled. The antidote for overapplying the antidote is known as resting in equanimity. In this case it's best to rest as you are.

For thousands of years, teachers have provided us with many tools, but it's up to us to learn how to use them. It takes experience and maturity to be intimate with the intricacies of our mind. We have to be able to see exactly what is going on: "Ah, I'm not just distracted, I'm stuck in elation." Then we can apply some practical advice. Working with obstacles like laxity and elation is a process of trial and error. Even as our practice is becoming subtler, we're still discovering the ways to hold our mind to the breath.

In fact, as we practice shamatha, most of the time we'll be learning how to recognize laxity and elation and then overcome them by applying the appropriate antidote. When a musician asked the Buddha how he should meditate, the Buddha asked him, "How do you tune the strings of your guitar?" The musician answered, "Not too tight, not too loose, so it makes the right sound." The Buddha said, "Similarly, you should hold your mind in meditation." Just as in playing a musical instrument, holding the mind "not too tight, not too loose" takes practice.

When our awareness is very strong, we can deal with obstacles as they arise while continuing to hold our mind to the breath. As soon as we detect an obstacle, we first relax our focus on the technique. We're still applying it, but it's not as clear, crisp, or tight. At the same time, we're able to deal with whatever trouble is arising. It's like answering the phone while we're cooking.

In this way the meditation continues without being interrupted. It's not as if we stop, deal with the obstacle, and come back. This is how awareness begins to extend the process of mindfulness. The combination of mindfulness and awareness is like walking across the room holding a cup full of water. Mindfulness maintains the proper angle and degree of pressure; awareness makes sure that it doesn't spill.

Mindfulness is a helpful tool; in the chaos of our daily life, we need to be mindful of many things. It's awareness, however, that becomes the bridge between the cushion and our everyday life. Who's paying attention to how we're using our body, speech, and mind as we move through the day? Awareness. With awareness we can understand our conduct in any situation. It's how we know we're being a jerk and need to be more kind. It's how we know we're scared or fearful—or fear*less*. It is this knowing quality of awareness that will ultimately lead to the development of our enlightened mind.

Eleven

Nine Stages of Training the Mind

As the lineage of meditators sat on their cushions and worked with their minds, they saw the same unfolding process: nine ways that the mind can be true to its inherent stability, clarity, and strength. In their descriptions of nine stages of training the mind, they left us signposts of that process. These guidelines are helpful because the mind is so vast that if we're left to our own devices, we'll usually just wander in thought. These nine stages are a map of the meditative process.

The first four stages—placement, continual placement, repeated placement, and close placement—have to do with developing stability. Stages five and six— taming and pacifying—have to do with developing clarity. And the last three stages—thoroughly pacifying, one-pointed, and equanimity—have to do with building strength.

1. Placement

Placing our mind on the breath is the first thing we do in meditation. In the moment of placing our mind, we're mounting the horse: we put our foot in the stirrup and pull ourselves up to the saddle. It's a matter of taking our seat properly.

This moment of placement starts when we extract our mind from its engagement with events, problems, thoughts, and emotions. We take that wild and busy mind and place it on the breath. Even though we're placing our consciousness, which isn't physical, placement feels very physical. It's as deliberate as placing a rock on top of a leaf.

In order for placement to be successful, we have to formally acknowledge that we're letting go of concepts, thoughts, and emotions: "Now I'm placing my mind upon the breath." What happens in that moment? Our attachments are uprooted. If we can even attempt such a thing, our discursiveness is greatly reduced. At the same time, by placing it on the breath, we're gathering that mind that's spread thin all over.

For beginning meditators the first stage is where we learn how to balance the focus on breathing, recognition of thoughts, and holding the posture. It's a grace period during which we develop good meditation habits. As we continue in our practice, placement is always the first step. It's that moment at the beginning of each session when we recognize and acknowledge that we've begun meditating. Because it establishes our attitude toward the rest of the session, it's the most important stage. The moment of placement gives our meditation a crisp, clean start. If we begin in a vague or ambiguous way, then our meditation will only continue to be vague and ambiguous. Like placing a domino, how carefully we place our mind in the first stage will directly affect the development of the next.

After that first moment, each time you choose to recognize and acknowledge a thought and return your consciousness to the breath, you're learning placement. It's such a small act, so innocuous, but it's one of the most courageous things you can do. When you recognize and release that thought, you can take pride in yourself. You've overcome laziness. You've remembered the instructions. You can feel happy coming back to the breath. Don't worry that you're going to have to do it again—you're going to do it thousands of times. That's why this is called practice.

Each time you remember to place your mind on the breath, you're moving forward. Just by letting a thought go, you're extracting yourself from concepts, negative emotions, and bewilderment. You're letting go of the need to be endlessly entertained and consumed. You have to do it again and again and again. Change happens one breath at a time, one thought at a time. Each time you return to the breath, you're taking one step away from addiction to discursiveness and fear and one step forward on the path of enlightenment, beginning with developing compassion for yourself.

I love golf. I play it whenever I can. No matter what kind of game I'm having, I can hit only one ball at a time. Each ball is the only ball; my mind has to be fresh every time. If I think of the balls I've hit or the balls I will hit, I'm not really hitting *this* ball. I'm only ingraining bad habits. It's the same with placement. If you're not crisp and fresh in recognizing and releasing thoughts, you're not really meditating; you're ingraining sloppiness. Those thoughts will gain power, and eventually you won't be meditating at all. You'll just be thinking.

Recognizing, acknowledging, and releasing a thought is like reaching the top of a mountain. It's worthy of the warrior's cry, *"Ki ki so so!"* What we celebrate is leaving behind the self-indulgent fantasies that will rob us of our life unless we work with them properly. Inspiration, view, effort, trust, mindfulness, and awareness support us in this.

The more we're able to gather our attention and focus, the stronger our mind becomes, the stronger the experience becomes, and the stronger the result becomes. We know we're able to place our minds properly when we can hold our focus on the breathing for roughly twenty-one cycles without our mind becoming enormously distracted.

2. Continual Placement

Placing our mind on the breath is now fairly easy. We've learned to mount the horse, and now we feel comfortable being in the saddle. The horse is walking along the trail. We're experiencing how it feels to be on the breath, to be continually in placement. When discursiveness and distraction take us off the trail, by and large we're able to implement placement to get back on. What allows us to do this is further development of mindfulness and awareness, lack of laziness, and remembering the instructions.

Another reason we're able to successfully place our mind on the breath is that we have confidence in the reasons why we're meditating. We do it with enthusiasm because we know it will bring us peace. We see the futility of outside concerns, fantasies, thoughts, and emotions. We're willing to give them up at least for the period of our meditation because we see the benefits of doing so. Placement has become a reasonable thing to do.

When resting our mind on the breathing and relating to our thoughts with ease becomes the norm, we're coming to the end of this stage. A benchmark is that we're able to rest our minds for roughly 108 cycles of the breath without being caught in distraction. Through 108 breaths—in and out—we can be mindful of the breathing. Although we may experience some discursiveness, the thoughts aren't bothersome or large enough that we lose mindfulness and forget the breathing altogether.

At this stage our mindfulness and stability last only so long; then our mind drifts off. But when the mainstay of our practice is that we can stay on the breathing for 108 breaths, giving ourselves a little wiggle room in that we will be neither completely still nor completely distracted, then we've graduated from the second to the third stage, which is known as repeated placement.

3. Repeated Placement

We might feel like we have been doing "repeated placement" since the beginning. But the landscape of meditation is vast, and the stages progressively subtle, because they describe our experience, which becomes more and more refined. The Tibetan word for this stage is *len*, which means to retrieve, to gather, to bring back. We've learned how to place our mind and how to continue to place our mind, but occasionally a thought still breaks out like a wild horse galloping across the plains.

In the first two stages this happened incessantly. By the third stage it happens only occasionally.

During the second stage, we learned to enjoy the ride. We're delighted that we can stay in the saddle and enjoy the scenery. In the third stage we become more confident. But the horse still has spontaneous moments of excitement and wildness. Now and then it rears or bucks or leaves the trail. We have to bring it back. We practice occasionally retrieving it throughout the third stage, and by the end we do it less and less. Our mindfulness is maturing into stability.

Now we're able to focus on our breathing, on being present. When the mind departs, it's usually to chase fantasies of little pleasures, from food to better weather to romantic adventures. This is elation: we're holding our mind too tightly. We're focused on the breath so hard that the mind suddenly departs. As this stage progresses, the speed and efficiency with which we retrieve our mind increases. By comparison, the way we extracted ourselves from thoughts in earlier stages looks messy. Sometimes it was like quicksand—the harder we tried to get out, the more we were embroiled. But now, because mindfulness is so strong, we're able to remove ourselves with precision. By the end of this stage we've achieved one of the milestones of shamatha: stability. Mindfulness is so potent that we're able to remain on the breath without ever being fully distracted. Awareness is also becoming more astute. We're beginning to catch thoughts before they occur.

Our meditation isn't as clear and vibrant as it could be, but it feels good and peaceful because we've stabilized our minds. Throughout the course of a session, our mind always remains in the theater of meditation. This is an admirable accomplishment. In Tibet it is likened to a vulture soaring high in the sky over a dead animal. This bird now always keeps its eye on the food. It may drift a little to the left or right, but it never loses sight of the food. Similarly our minds may drift here and there, but never away from the breath.

Before the end of the third stage, sometimes we were present for our practice and sometimes we weren't. Now we're there for all of it. This is stability. It didn't happen because we hit ourselves over the head with an overly simplified meditation technique. We achieved it gently and precisely through repetition, consistency, view, attitude, intention, proper posture, and good surroundings.

4. Close Placement

The entry to the fourth stage, which is known as close placement, is marked by nondistraction. We always remain close to the breath. That's when we know we've crossed the border. This is stability. We know that even though the horse will wander here and there, it won't be leaving the trail.

Our meditation now takes on a different twist. Previously our main concern was not to be distracted from the breath. We were worried that our mind was going to be sucked back into everyday problems. We were always wondering if we'd be strong enough to return to the breath. Now we're more relaxed. We're no longer wondering if we can stay on the breath because we know we can. We're no longer concerned about outside influences pulling us away from meditation because we know they won't. Our confidence is heightened. Now we're concerned about the quality of our meditation—the texture, the experience. Before we were worried that we couldn't get a cup of coffee; now we want a mocha cappuccino. How can we make our minds stronger, more vibrant? This is our new priority.

By and large, we've overcome the obstacles of laziness and forgetting the instructions. These obstacles were bad because they kept us from meditating. By the end of the third stage and into the fourth stage we're dealing with the obstacles of elation and laxity. Either extreme has distracting results. However, since by now we're always remaining at the scene of our practice, these are considered good problems to have.

In Tibet we're warned that at the fourth stage we might be fool enough to think we've achieved enlightenment or high realization—the mind feels so strong and stable and good. Because the struggle with our mind has been reduced greatly, there's a quality of joy and ease. But if we enjoy the stability of the mind too much, it will become too relaxed. We might not reach the other stages. Hence the obstacle of laxity. Our mind is stable but not clear. The bird can't land on the meat; it can only fly around it. We need awareness to home in, sharpen sensibility, pull our mind in tighter.

5. Taming

Even though the accomplishments at the third and fourth stages are heroic, there's further to go. In the fifth stage we're able to tighten up our meditation by bringing in more clarity. This stage is known as taming because we begin to experience the true fruits of a tamed mind, something that we began to cultivate long ago in the first stage. Taming here is the experience of *lesu rungwa,* being able to make our mind workable. In the fourth stage, we might still feel awed by the fact that we've tamed the horse. But now a strong, stable, and clear mind feels natural. Our mind is not perfectly still. We still have discursive thoughts. But we're feeling true synergy with the horse. We're feeling harmony. We're no longer struggling.

The harmony and synergy create joy. A traditional metaphor for what we experience at this stage is the delight of a bee drawing nectar from a flower. Meditation tastes good, joyous. If you've ever had a hard time and then suddenly felt the pressure lift, you might have briefly known such bliss and liberation.

6. Pacifying

The sixth stage is known as pacifying. A great battle has taken place and there is victory. We're seated on the horse surveying the field. We know we've won. We feel tranquil and vibrant like mountain greenery after a thunderstorm. Everything has been watered and energized. There is tremendous clarity.

We're still working with a mind that is sometimes tight and sometimes loose. In our practice we still have to make many little adjustments. But in making these adjustments we're no longer frantic, as we might have been in the first few stages. Then it was questionable that we would ever make our mind an ally, and now the peace we feel tells us that we have. Our meditation is joyous and clear. We begin to experience not only mind's natural harmony, but also its inherent strength.

At this stage we also feel excitement. We begin to see the possibilities of what we can accomplish with our tamed mind. Before, this relationship was a burden, but now it's full of possibilities. The wild horse has been tamed.

7. Thoroughly Pacifying

The battle may be over, but there are still a few little enemy soldiers running around in the form of subtle thoughts, mostly about pleasure. We may be slightly attached to how good meditation feels. There are little dualistic rumblings. Although we know that they're not going to disrupt our meditation, we can't just sit back and ignore them. In thoroughly pacifying, we don't dispel the thoughts as we did in stage four. Now we seduce them, like snow falling into fire. Our meditation is becoming so strong that when thoughts and emotions encounter its heat they naturally dissolve.

Remember the waterfall of thoughts we felt when we first sat down on the cushion to tame our minds? It's become a lake with only a few little ripples.

8. One-Pointed

By the eighth stage, known as one-pointed, the remnants of discursiveness have evaporated. We're sitting there completely awake, clear, and knowing. This is possible because we're no longer distracted. Our meditation has developed all the attributes of perfection, which is what we will accomplish at the ninth stage. The only difference is that at the beginning of meditation we still have to make a slight effort to point our mind in the direction of the breath.

9. Equanimity

Our meditation has come to perfection. When we sit down we engage with the breath in a completely fluid and spontaneous manner. Our mind is strong, stable, clear, and joyous. We feel a complete sense of victory. We could meditate forever. Even in the back of our mind, there are no traces of thoughts. We're in union with the present moment. Our mind is at once peaceful and powerful, like a mountain. There's a sense of equanimity.

This is perfection. Like a finely trained racehorse, our mind remains motionless but alive with energy. The mind has actually grown—in strength as well as size. We feel magnanimous, expansive. This is the fruition of peaceful abiding. Now we have a mind that is able to focus in any endeavor. We feel centered and confident.

Three

TURNING THE
MIND INTO
AN ALLY

Twelve

Turning the Mind

The power of peaceful abiding is that we begin to see how our mind works. We begin to see how our life works, too. That changes us. When we first began to practice, we might have felt as though thoughts and emotions were solid. Our minds were weak. Thoughts and emotions seemed overwhelming. Now we see that they're like mist rising from water. We see that thoughts are powerful because we believe in them, so much so that we base our entire life on them. How we dress, what we eat, where we live, and everything else about our life is a product of our thinking. What were we thinking when we bought this? What were we thinking when we did that? We begin to see how our belief in the solidity of thoughts has created this concept called "me." We see that at the basis of our being is something deeper and more open than fantasies, emotions, and discursiveness.

Now thoughts don't have the power over us that they did before. We're not distracted. Our mindfulness and awareness are keen. Through consistent practice, we've grown familiar with the feeling of a focused mind. We've developed the strength to stay with it. This state of clarity connects us with reality. Whether we're writing a master's thesis or cooking a meal, we're clear about who we are and what we're doing. We know our basic goodness. The mind's our ally, and we feel wholesome and complete. It's as if we've slept well and eaten well, and we're in good surroundings. We have a healthy sense of self.

With a healthy sense of self we feel at ease. Everything we need is already here. We're centered within a state of contentment. We're not too hard on ourselves; at the same time, we're wise to our own little tricks. We know how we get slippery. We know when we're trying to get away with something. We're comfortable looking at ourselves honestly. Our mind is open and supple. We're becoming inquisitive because a whole range of reality we hadn't noticed before is coming into focus. With this openness, flexibility, and curiosity, we begin to see certain truths about the way things are.

The Buddha taught that to wake up from the dream of bewilderment and suffering, we first need to sit still and take a deep breath. Peaceful abiding is that deep breath, a way to strip away the chaos of bewilderment and find some basic sanity. But peaceful abiding is only the beginning of the spiritual journey. Simply withdrawing into the stability of our own minds could turn meditation practice into just another way to shop for pleasure. Instead, with this healthy sense of self we can look more deeply into the meaning of our being. We can take meditation further by using insight, *vipashyana* in Sanskrit, to reflect accurately on our own experience and on the nature of existence. We can point our mind in a new direction—away from illusions and toward reality. We do this through the practice of contemplation.

In a nutshell, the emotions we experience all come down to passion, aggression, and bewilderment. With peaceful abiding we've been working mostly with seeing how we're either grasping what we want—passion—or pushing away what we don't want—aggression. This is like clearing the field of vines and thorn bushes. Now we have a stable mind that sees clearly the distractions of these two powerful forces and has the strength not to be swayed by them. What we're left with is the power of ignorance, and ignorance is the source of suffering. Ignorance is like a deeply rooted weed with runners. If we aren't aware of the pitfalls of delusion, how can we deal with them? We can dismantle our illusions by contemplating the reality of human life and our potential to awaken the mind of enlightenment. This is what we do in contemplative meditation.

I've said that our bewildered mind is like a wild horse. I have a very high regard for horses. When I was in high school, I spent some time working on a ranch in West Texas. A stallion in the distance on the high plains is a powerful sight to behold. We don't tame such a strong majestic creature by beating the spirit out it. Instead, we work with its raw power and turn that energy in a certain direction. Where do we want to take that horse? Where do we want to go riding? We want to make a real journey. We want to ride in the meadows of compassion, the gardens of awakened heart, the fields of wisdom. This is the essence of the practice of contemplation: we learn to direct the energy of our mind toward enlightenment.

When we practice shamatha, we gather the energy of the mind by drawing it in. We disempower bewilderment by recognizing and releasing thoughts and emotions. Initially thoughts are a problem because we're so distracted by them. They're a problem when they build into strong emotions, because they destabilize us. In contemplative meditation, we use them. Our object of meditation is no longer the breath. Instead, we hold our mind to a thought or a sentence and keep it there, and use insight to understand its meaning. This brings our concepts more in tune with reality.

The Buddha was considered to be a renegade because he asked people to look in this way at the truth of what was going on. He left us clues about the nature of reality and how to encourage the mind of enlightenment — "precious human birth," "impermanence," "death," "karma," "samsara," and "awakened heart or mind." What do these words really mean? How can we let them penetrate our being and allow us to transform? Contemplating the meaning of a particular thought moves us from concept toward a direct experience of reality, which is wisdom.

We can say "blue," but until we see the color blue, we don't really know what the meaning is. We can say that something is hot, but until we touch it, we don't know what "hot" means. We can talk about bringing our mind to compassion by saying "May all sentient beings be free from suffering and the root of suffering," but until we feel the pain of others, "pain" is only a word. We have to crack its shell to let its meaning infuse us, seep into our lives.

In contemplative meditation we are getting to the inner essence of reality. After a certain point, the words fall away, but the meaning stays. We are no longer operating from the basis of concept. The subject-object separation is gone. The reality of birth, death, impermanence, and free and well-favored human birth has penetrated us. Just like the Buddha after he left the palace, we've incorporated their reality. We've picked the fruit off the tree and we can finally drink the juice. That's the point of contemplation—hearing, listening, understanding. It puts us in tune with the nature of things.

Seeing through ignorance and realizing the meaning of our lives is very precise work—work for a mind that is stable, clear, and strong. It takes patience to do this practice. As my father used to say, it's like combing our hair over and over again. We're becoming familiar with thoughts that will shift the stream of our being, the direction of our lives—if we let their meaning penetrate us. In becoming familiar with love and compassion, karma and samsara, the preciousness of being human, the inevitability of death, we train in diving deep into the truth and awakening our dormant wisdom.

Contemplative Meditation Instructions

Since having a stable mind is the ground of contemplation, begin your session with a few minutes of shamatha. Then shift your focus from the breath to a certain thought, inspiration, or intent. For example, you can

say to yourself, "Now I am placing my mind on the preciousness of human birth." Or "Now I am placing my
mind on the reality of impermanence." Then gather the
mind and place it on those words. Contemplation is
peaceful abiding with a different object, so everything
you've learned about shamatha applies to this practice.
When you recognize that you're thinking about something besides the object of meditation, acknowledge
that you're distracted and return to the thought you're
contemplating.

In this practice, the words are the gateway to the
meaning. As you continue to place your mind on them,
eventually the words fall away and their meaning or
the experience to which they refer will arise. For example, you may start to feel your heart opening as you
wish that your sister or your best friend be happy. In
contemplating impermanence or death, you might feel
a sense of groundlessness. By resting your mind in that
meaning, that feeling, you're building familiarity with a
particular facet of reality.

At times you may find that you place your mind on
the words and you don't really feel a thing. Just continue resting your mind on the words. As your own
relationship with those words deepens, eventually an
experience of their meaning will arise. It's sometimes
necessary to really *think* about what you're doing.
Return to the words as the object of meditation, and at

SAKYONG MIPHAM

the same time, bring in thoughts, images, and memories to enrich your contemplation. Sometimes I'll remember the beggars I've seen in India, for example, to help evoke a feeling of compassion. If you're practicing raising the mind of love, you can imagine people you know being really happy. This kind of focused and controlled thinking can crack the shell of the words and let the meaning come through.

At the end of your session, let the meaning of your meditation become your view. For example, if you've been contemplating the preciousness of human birth, throughout the day you can let your mind rest in a sense of appreciation for life. You can be thoroughly soaked in the message of your contemplation.

The topics in the following chapters are helpful to contemplate at some point in your practice. They will help you ground yourself in the realities of your life, appreciate what you have, and utilize your insight to go beyond the boundaries of "me." You can also use these contemplations as antidotes if you're feeling a lack of courage or if you're feeling disheartened. They will give you inspiration. For example, when you feel that things are falling apart, you can contemplate the preciousness of human life to remind yourself of what you have. When you feel that you're making emotions and thoughts solid, you can contemplate impermanence to remind yourself that everything is in flux. When you're

136

in the throes of an intense situation, you can contemplate the nature of samsara instead of feeling that you're completely to blame. When you're in the grips of anger or desire, it can be helpful to contemplate and dismantle the emotion according to the instruction given in Chapter 6.

You can contemplate these topics at any time. First do a little sitting, and then turn your mind to the contemplation of your choice for ten minutes or so. At the end of the contemplation, sit for a few more minutes. Depending on your schedule and how the practice feels, do one topic a day, one a week, or even one a month. In an all-day session of practice, you could do one topic in the morning and another in the afternoon.

For a summary of instructions for contemplative meditation, see Appendix C.

Thirteen

The Joy of
Being Human

In turning the mind into an ally, we are actively encouraging virtue — *gewa* in Tibetan. We can think of virtue as the qualities of an enlightened being, our enlightened genetic makeup. We are being courageous like a warrior in strengthening these positive aspects of ourselves. They include a stable mind, a healthy sense of self grounded in the experience of basic goodness, a clear view of the facts of life, an unconditionally loving heart, and the wisdom to know the right thing to do at all times. The mind of enlightenment sees things as they are. An enlightened being sees a noncompounded truth that is empty, joyous, and luminous — the basic nature of all. What the Buddha discovered on his journey is that we're all ultimately capable of seeing this truth and consciously rooting our activities in it. Our potential is to become totally happy.

Perhaps we think of enlightenment as an instant transformation. One minute the Buddha was sitting under the tree, a regular Joe from India, and the next minute he woke up as Shakyamuni Buddha, the Totally Blessed One. However, it didn't happen like that. Enlightenment was the tail end of a long process. The Buddha was diligent in training and developing his mind. It took exertion, patience, and discipline to transform himself this way.

Like spring bulbs dormant underneath the frozen earth, the qualities of the enlightened mind need time and the proper conditions to grow. Although surprising and revealing moments of insight may deepen our understanding, the mind of enlightenment doesn't open in an instant. These moments of insight are like the days getting warmer and longer at the end of winter. One warm sunny day isn't going to make the flowers bloom, but as more of them occur, we're going to see signs of stems and leaves and eventually buds. Just so, as our moments of insight accumulate, they begin to influence our activity; we're able to open our hearts. We begin to use what we've understood in contemplation to inspire our conduct in the world. The kind of insights we're going to have and our ability to know their meaning will depend on the strength of mind that we've already established.

Most of us contemplate what's missing in our lives,

as opposed to what we have. Contemplating what we have opens up our mind to be bigger, less insular. In contemplating the joy of being human, we focus on the words, "Joyful human birth, difficult to find, free and well favored."

When I was young, I used to entertain myself this way before falling asleep. In my mind's eye I would see myself lying in bed. I would zoom back like a camera to include my house in my neighborhood in Boulder, in Colorado, in the United States of America, on the continent of North America. Then I would look at the planet like a globe, including India, where I was born; Tibet, where my father and mother were born; and Scotland, where I learned to speak English. Then I would picture Earth as a beautiful blue sphere floating in blackness. I would make the picture bigger, including other planets in our solar system with the sun in the center. The most amazing thing was to see earth disappearing into the darkness as a speck. Then I would imagine the outer planets of the solar system. The sun would disappear as I imagined all the stars in our galaxy, which seemed endless. I would dissolve our galaxy into one star, one light, and make that light very tiny, surrounded by other lights in the darkness, which weren't stars, but galaxies. Then I would think about how small I was, and how strange and wonderful it is to have been born.

Everybody we know was born. Everyone we see was once a baby. First they weren't here, and then they were. We don't often contemplate birth—we're too busy worrying about money, food, the way we look, the way other people look, what other people are thinking about the way we look. But birth is a profound passage. Seeing a chick pecking its way out of an egg is moving and powerful. Even though in being born we suffer, birth can happen in such love, such openness. And like death, birth shows us the fragility of life.

Of all the hundreds of millions of stars and planets just within our own little Milky Way, this seems to be the only one that can support life. The scientific proof we have of life elsewhere is in amino acids and rocks— not even in animals, much less human beings. If we think about how many other kinds of beings are born here on Earth, it's amazing that we're born human. A traditional Buddhist teaching on the difficulty of obtaining human birth uses the image of a blind tortoise swimming in an ocean that's as big as the earth, with an ox's yoke tossing on the surface. Once every five hundred years the turtle swims up to the surface. The chances of obtaining a human birth are said to be as small as the chances of that turtle emerging with its head in the yoke.

We can think about how free we are in the human realm. The Buddha saw it as *the* place to be, because in this realm—if we're lucky—we can hear and practice spiritual teachings. We can discover our natural state and help others discover theirs. Even though beings in other realms still have the possibility of awakened mind, by and large, it's more difficult to cultivate. According to the Buddhist teachings, in some of these realms, beings don't even have bodies. In others, they think they have a body but they don't. There are realms in which beings suffer too much to ever go beyond it. There are realms where they're constantly tortured by heat or cold or sharpness or wetness or dryness or brightness or darkness. There are realms where beings are totally consumed by jealousy or anger. There are realms where beings are always hungry. In other realms beings don't experience enough suffering to investigate reality; they're having too much fun. These are godlike realms where beings live for a long time—but not forever. There's also the realm of animals, where ignorance rules. Here there's less possibility of realizing awakened mind because all energy goes into trying to stay alive.

The habits of animals are pretty fascinating. When I watch a nature show on television, I wonder, "Do animals ever think about anything? If one beaver has a bigger tree to munch on, do the others get upset?" In contemplating the human realm, we can think about how animals suffer—how they're used as beasts of burden, how we eat them, how they eat each other. It seems that most of their lives are territorial and chaotic. There's incredible aggression, struggle, and fear in the animal realm. If we go camping in a place where there are dangerous animals, we know how it feels to have to worry about being eaten.

"Well favored" means that we've been born in a time and place where we have the luxury of hearing, contemplating, and putting into action teachings that awaken us to our enlightened mind. We're relatively healthy, we have a roof over our head and food in our mouths. We have family and friends. We've encountered someone who can teach us how to train our mind and open our heart. Being threatened by nuclear war, terrorism, and global warming is a reminder that we can't take such conditions for granted. We're just these tiny vulnerable beings riding on a blue dot in space. Yet sometimes we act as if we're the center of the universe. The enlightened alternative is to appreciate how incredibly rare and precious human life is. The enlightened alternative is to appreciate *everything*. By appreciating whatever we encounter, we can use it to further our journey of warriorship. We are good as we are, and it is good as it is. Once we have this understanding, we'll see that we are living in a sacred world.

As a result, we can be joyful. We may not be happy all day every day, but we won't feel so sorry for ourselves. Through appreciating every aspect of human life, we can benefit others. When we're in good health, we can appreciate that. When we're ill, we can use the illness to awaken to the preciousness of our lives. We can appreciate the health that we have and feel compassion for others who are more ill. Even when we're very ill, we can be curious and courageous, and use it as an opportunity to inspire others.

When we're in any kind of pain, we can use it to open our hearts to the reality that people are always suffering. Pain is something everyone experiences. We can use it to ground us in the fundamental truth of our being. Pain gives us firsthand experience by which to be kind and generous to others. It gives us direct access through our empathy to helping others. We can use pain to activate compassion. We'd like others not to experience pain, and we can extend ourselves to them. We can contemplate the words, "May all beings be free of pain." Our direct experience of pain only makes our wish more potent. It may even decrease our pain, because it increases our joy. This becomes a wonderful meditation, to sit there and contemplate the relief of pain and suffering of everyone, of the whole world — not only because it changes our attitude toward our own pain, but also because it's opening our mind of enlightenment. This kind of prayer is always healing.

If we're materially wealthy, we can appreciate the power it bestows on us to help others. If we're not wealthy, we can appreciate the simplicity and freedom of that. We can always contemplate and appreciate what we do have. In peaceful abiding we have the means by which to tame our wild-horse mind. In contemplation we have a way to rouse the courage to direct our mind toward enlightenment. When we generate selfless love and compassion, we manifest tremendous power to help others find freedom from the bewildering and claustrophobic darkness of samsara. We are indeed well favored.

These are just a few thoughts we might contemplate to fully experience the meaning of our precious human birth. As we practice turning our mind toward an appreciation of our basic situation, we become less enmeshed in self-involvement. It becomes easier to tune in to the simple and ordinary pleasures of our existence. Our problems become smaller. Because we appreciate what we have, being alive seems fresh and good.

Fourteen

The Unchanging
Truth of Change

The face of impermanence is constantly showing itself. Why do we struggle to hide it? Why do we feed the circle of suffering by perpetuating the myth of permanence? Experiences, friends, relationships, possessions, knowledge—we work so hard to convince ourselves that they will last. When a cup breaks or we forget something or somebody dies or the seasons change, we're surprised. We can't quite believe it's over.

Most summers I conduct a program at our retreat center in the Rocky Mountains. We create a world of tents in a huge meadow—dining tent, meditation tent, sleeping tents. It's refreshing to live like this, since most of us live in buildings all year round. At the beginning of the summer we put the tents up, and at the end we take them down. After the tents come down and we look into the meadow, we're always surprised. We feel happy and sad. We're happy in reflecting back on what occurred during the summer; we're sad that all the tents are gone. It seemed so real. No matter how many times we've done it, at the end of each summer we have the same feeling.

This bittersweet taste marks our lives. The movie ends, our relationship's over, children grow up. Impermanence is always pounding at the door. Of course, acknowledging impermanence doesn't mean we get permanence. It means we're more in tune with reality; we can relax. As we relinquish our attachment to permanence, pain begins to diminish because we're no longer fooled. Accepting impermanence means that we spend less energy resisting reality. Our suffering has a more direct quality. We're no longer trying to avoid it. We see that impermanence is a river that runs through life, not a rock that stands in the way. We see that because we resist impermanence, pain and suffering are constants. We realize that pain comes from our desire for permanence.

Contemplation helps us understand profound truths that we rarely consider, even though our life is contained by them. We contemplate these truths to bring about a shift in our understanding of reality, our perception of our life. When, during a meditation session, we hold our mind to the words "Everything is impermanent," the meaning begins to come through.

When we have a glimpse of impermanence, we hold our mind to that realization. In this way we become familiar with a simple truth that we may have overlooked. We begin to live our lives with a deeper understanding.

At this very instant the weather is changing, our hair is growing, people are dying and being born, and the earth is shifting on its axis as it circles round the sun. We're growing older. Perhaps our mood has changed since yesterday. No matter how clear this may be to our intellect, we tend to put ourselves into a trance, thinking things are permanent. We're hypnotized into thinking the world is permanent, we're permanent, relationships are permanent, feelings are permanent. But all of it is impermanent. This contemplation brings us to a very basic level of understanding. It brings us back to the middle of the saddle.

When I was eight, I flew from India to England. I had never been in an airplane before. As we began to land in London, looking down I saw a world of tiny buildings, tiny streets, and tiny cars and trucks. This delighted me. I couldn't wait for the plane to land so that I could drive one of those little cars. But as we landed, that little world suddenly grew to adult proportions. It changed.

The world is made of infinite moving parts. The mind produces a seeming continuity of events and

ideas. What we call "war" is a series of calamities arising from beliefs and opinions, which are always subject
to change. What we call "peace" is the absence of
aggression, a tenuous state. When it is winter, summer
no longer exists. We organize our life around the concept of a solid self in a solid world, even though all of it
is simply ideas and forms coming in and out of existence, like thousands of stars flickering in the night. Is
there anything that is not impermanent?

In contemplating impermanence we can consider
what permanence would mean. Permanence would be
awkward. It would be an unchanging situation, isolated in space, unaffected by time or the elements.
There would be no beginning and no end, no causes
and conditions. Everything would last forever. There'd
be no seasons. We'd never be born, grow up, fall in
love, have children, grow old, or die. We'd never eat
because we'd never be hungry. We couldn't be in relationship to anything else, because it would change us.
In contemplating impermanence, we see the impossi-
bility of life being anything other than what it is. We
begin to lighten up and enjoy the constant play of light
and dark, of visible and invisible, of increase and
decrease.

Contemplating impermanence can be a liberating
experience, one that brings both sobriety and joy. In
essence, we become less attached. We realize we can't

really have anything. We have money and then it's gone; we have sadness and then it's gone. No matter how we want to cling to our loved ones, by nature every relationship is a meeting and a parting. This doesn't mean we have less love. It means we have less fixation, less pain. It means we have more freedom and appreciation, because we can relax into the ebb and flow of life.

Understanding the meaning of impermanence makes us less desperate people. It gives us dignity. We no longer grasp at pleasure, trying to squeeze out every last drop. We no longer consider pain something we should fear, deny, and avoid. We know that it will change. This is a very strong direction toward opening the mind of enlightenment. We've learned to look at what's in front of us. We don't have to keep imitating an idea of permanent happiness: "If I work hard, I'm going to make a lot of money, and then I'll be happy." We see that happiness doesn't come about that way; it comes from cultivating the virtues that lead to enlightenment. Ultimately, it comes from wisdom, from understanding the unchanging truth of change.

Fifteen

First We Get Old

In a society as enamored of youth as ours, it is helpful to contemplate the process of aging. If we think about it and understand its place in our life, we can change our attitude toward aging. In this contemplation we place our mind on the meaning of the words "Aging is the nature of the human condition. I celebrate it."

Birth is a painful and wonderful event. From that moment on, we age. As a child we experience the pains of growing, of not knowing anything, of making friends in a newfound world. As an adolescent, we go through the pains of peer pressure and puberty. It all passes very quickly. When we're young, we want to be older. When we're older, perhaps we wish we were younger.

During the millennium celebrations, I watched a series of interviews with people who had lived for a hundred years or more. Each of them was asked, "If you could relive any period of your life, when would it be?" Universally, they said it would be their sixties. At that age they had maturity of mind, and at the same time they still had a body that could do what they wanted. One of them had started running marathons in his sixties, another had taken flying lessons.

In terms of cultures, I straddle two worlds. In the West we fret about aging. We feel old, and we start acting old. In Tibet people don't seem to worry as much about aging. When I hear my mother and her generation of Tibetans talk about getting old, the tone in their voice is proud. They're proud to have lived so long. They're cheerful. They have young minds. They're continuously curious, always learning. One of my favorite Tibetan sayings is "Even if you're going to die tomorrow, you can learn something tonight." With this attitude we don't feel so old.

Once when I was driving home from the airport with my mother late at night, we passed McDonald's. I said, "That's the most famous restaurant in America." She said, "That one?" I explained that there are many McDonald's restaurants and that many people don't approve of the food they serve. She said she wanted to give it a try. Since she mostly eats traditional Tibetan food, I didn't think she would like it. We took the drive-through at McDonald's, which was a brand-new experience for her. The whole process amazed her. I ordered her a burger, and as we drove away, she took her first bite. I asked her how she liked it. To my surprise and horror, she said, "It's perfect! The meat is hot, and the bread is soft." It turns out that she doesn't like many restaurants in America, but she loves McDonald's.

In contemplating aging, perhaps we'll take a hint from our Tibetan friends and enjoy and appreciate growing old, as opposed to dreading it. We don't have to squeeze all the life out of our existence in an attempt to overcome the process of getting older. We can age with dignity. As we age we're wiser, more experienced; we have more wisdom to offer others. We can maintain our health and vitality with the right activity, food, and most of all, curiosity about life. We can learn to celebrate the truth of aging without hiding in the shadows of denial and discursiveness.

Sixteen

And Then We Die

We spend most of our time avoiding death, not thinking about it. When we do, it gives us the shivers. We might feel slightly surprised, knocked off balance. We're afraid of death, partly because we don't know what will happen, partly because we're afraid of the pain we might feel when it happens. When we peek into the door of death by contemplating it, its meaning begins to penetrate us. Contemplating death gives us strength because it liberates our fear. So we contemplate the meaning of these words: "Death is my friend, my truest of friends, for it is always waiting for me."

All around us life and death are performing a dance that brings texture to our existence. Death is our friend because it gives us life. Death defines life. If we didn't have death, we might not appreciate life. In every moment of our life, death is waiting for us. We're going to die. We don't know when we're going to die; we don't know how we're going to die. Everyone we know is going to die—our parents, our friends, our children, our pets, people we like, people we don't like, kings and queens, heads of state, movie stars, rock stars, rich people, poor people. All have the same fate. This body will be a corpse.

Without being morbid about it, whenever death presents itself we can contemplate it. We can discuss it with our friends. If we come close to being hit by a bus, if we hurt ourselves in a car accident, if we get sick, we can ponder the permeable membrane between our life and our death. When someone close to us dies, we can look into death, question death, and let it transform us. "What is death about? Why is this happening?" Different traditions explain death in different ways. But when we experience the reality of death, it touches our life. It presents us with a deep mystery. Most of the time we might rather not investigate it. When we're directly under its influence, we can be open to it, try to understand it.

When I heard that my father was gravely ill, it just wouldn't sink in that he was probably going to die. He was a great meditation master and Buddhist teacher. After the Chinese invaded Tibet, he escaped on foot, leading three hundred people over the mountains into India. He spent many years of his life planting the flower of dharma on the rock of North America. He was a master warrior. If anyone could elude death, it seemed like it would be him. His death would leave a huge hole in my life as well as the lives of many others.

I was standing right next to him in the moment when he finally died. The space became very powerful and strong, almost luminous. There were no thoughts occurring. For days it was like that, as if reality had shifted. My whole life I had heard about death, had seen people who were dying and people who had died. But my father's death struck me in a different way. His mortality made me realize my own mortality. It made me realize everybody's mortality. It shook me out of my misconceptions. It profoundly changed my attitude. For many months I thought about how I was going to live the rest of my life. I realized that death is real. I mustn't waste time. I became much more dedicated to practice and study. Having this intimate experience of death helped me appreciate my life.

We often conduct our life as though it's going to last forever. With this attitude, we want everything. The fact of death puts a limit on what we can have, what we can do. We don't need to think about death all the time, but to ponder it, to contemplate it, gives us perspective and inspiration about living our life. It also makes us less spoiled. It makes us look at the balance of our life and determine what needs to come first. What is important to me? How shall I use my life? We're able to enter situations more openly once we've related with death. It makes our love more powerful.

Seventeen

Samsara and Karma

Everything we experience, all the ups and downs of our life, is fundamentally encapsulated in the word *samsara.* Samsara is a wheel that is endlessly spinning. We think that life progresses in a straight line pointed in the direction of improvement, but in fact we're in a circle of illusion that keeps us ending up just where we started. Karma, the action of cause and effect, is what keeps us here. No matter who we are, we're caught in this process.

Samsara always has to have the last word. We need one more thing to make us happy. One thing leads to the next, perpetuated by our desire to have final satisfaction. But the next experience feels uneasy, and we still need one more thing. We need to eat, then we need to listen to music, then we need to watch a movie, then we need to relax in a bath. The desire to feel satisfied is a continual process that drives our lives, and the end result is suffering. Samsara is not a sin; it's just what ends up happening when we're driven by negative emotions. What ends up happening is called suffering. From the perspective of the Buddha, we keep ourselves on this wheel lifetime after lifetime.

The suffering of samsara exhibits itself in three particular ways: the suffering of suffering, the suffering of change, and all-pervasive suffering. The suffering of suffering is very basic. Even being born into this life is painful. We cry because we have to leave our mother's body. Then we're brought into a world of heat and cold. To some degree we spend our whole life fortifying ourselves against these fundamental forms of suffering. Either we're putting on warm clothes to fight off the cold or building shelters to protect ourselves from the sun. With the suffering of suffering, we just can't win. We're late for a meeting, we lock our keys in the house, we cut our finger trying to get back in, then we get stuck in traffic, and when we finally arrive we discover that the meeting's been cancelled. That's the suffering of suffering.

Then there's the suffering of change. Whatever our object of pleasure, it changes to pain. We experience this kind of suffering when we fall in and out of love. We experience it when we eat a delicious meal at a great new restaurant and then several hours later find ourselves in the bathroom with churning bowels and a stomachache. We experience it when the clothes we buy are no longer fashionable. We experience it when our own body, which has been our continual basis for pleasure, gets sick, falls apart, and nags us with its needs. This is the suffering of change.

The third kind of suffering is all-pervasive suffering. It stems from the reality that nothing is solid, that everything is conditioned and in flux. At an atomic level, everything is coming and going all the time. Consciousness itself is coming in and out of existence hundreds of times in the snap of a finger. The world we perceive and how we perceive it is constantly changing. All-pervasive suffering is the inherent quality of this very process. No matter what we have, we can't fight the constant fluctuation and instability of existence. This level of instability brings mental agitation.

The point of contemplating samsara is not to feel overwhelmed or depressed, but to wake up to what samsara is and stop being fooled by it. Then we can give up trying to outwit samsara. We can give up the attitude that one of our schemes will result in permanent pleasure. We can recognize samsara, rise above it, and emerge from it. When we wake up in the morning we can tell ourselves that even though we'll experience suffering today, we don't need to be drawn into chasing our own tail trying to outsmart samsara.

Samsara isn't a place, it's an attitude: "I'm real and everything's for me." When we become aware of this attitude and what creates it, we can start to change it. What creates samsara is that we keep trying to get pleasure by engaging in nonvirtuous activity resulting from bewilderment, fixation, desire, aggression, jealousy, and pride. This leads not to pleasure but to suffering.

Suffering is the karma of nonvirtuous activity. Karma means "action." In Tibetan we say *le*. We tend to simplify the dynamic of karma by saying that one thing causes another. However, karma is more complex than that. There are many causes to any one effect. Think of all the conditions that must fall into place just for us to drive to work: good health, clothes to wear, a working car, no accidents on the way, knowing where the office is. Whatever happens is the result of many causes and conditions. Who grew the apple we eat? Who picked it? Who delivered it to the grocery store? Karma makes the world go round.

We all want to be happy. No one wants to suffer. So the point of contemplating karma is to look at what causes and conditions come together to produce happiness, and what causes and conditions come together to produce suffering. Then we can point ourselves in the direction of happiness.

If we're engaged in aggression and greed for the purpose of making our life better, the end result will be pain. If that pain leads to further anger and jealousy, we shouldn't be surprised; it's just karma in action. Conversely, actions based on virtues such as compassion, kindness, love, patience, and nonattachment lead to happiness. These are considered virtues because they elevate the mind above negative emotions. For example, if we practice nonaggression when we feel irritated with our spouse, instead of aggravating the situation with anger, we can resolve our differences peacefully and maintain harmony. Even though our patience may not be completely free of self-interest, nonetheless acting with virtue takes us toward the mind of enlightenment. By exercising virtue we'll eventually discover selflessness, emptiness, and luminosity. Acting from virtue leads to virtue, which leads to happiness.

If we plant peaches, we're always going to get peaches. If we plant pears, we're always going to get pears. Karma works in just this way. If you plant nonvirtue—*migewa*—you get suffering. If you plant virtue—*gewa*—you get happiness. If we're using strong negative emotions to get what we want, and what we want is happiness, it's never going to work. Therefore we need to contemplate our intentions and actions. Contemplating samsara and karma strengthens our intention to point our life away from suffering and toward true happiness.

Eighteen

Jumping into the Heart of the Buddha

When we contemplate impermanence, illness, aging, death—and all the other aspects of our precious human birth, we see how fixated we are, how strong-willed and tenacious we've been about our version of reality. It's clear that this fixation has caused us suffering and pain: the more self-involved we are, the more anger, jealousy, pride, and other traumatic emotions we have. Whenever we seek more self-satisfaction, we end up with more suffering, from minor to extreme. In every case the suffering results from some kind of selfish intent. We see that we've acted this way because we took our emotions, concepts, and thoughts to be real. Through the power of our meditation, we also see that these emotions are fundamentally illusory and empty. We've sat through hours of being angry and hours of being desirous and at the end it was all like a dream. It becomes clear to us that this simple misunderstanding is working against our happiness and well-being.

This is just what we need to open the mind of enlightenment: clear insight into the dynamics of bewilderment and suffering. We have to understand the nature of suffering and the origin of suffering. Once we do this, we've got the perspective of an enlightened being, which gives us a window to the world. We see that everyone wants to be happy, just like us, and that other beings also are creating a tremendous amount of pain and suffering based on illusory experiences that they take to be real. We begin to feel a genuine empathy with the suffering they're experiencing. We want their suffering to cease.

This is the birth of compassion. Compassion enlarges our heart. The Tibetan word for compassion is *nyingje*. *Nying* means essence, or heart. *Je* means lord, noble. Compassion is having the mind of the noble heart. Those of the noble-hearted family are warrior bodhisattvas, who have superior view and intention because their hearts are big and courageous. They want to do something about others' suffering.

Compassion gives rise to love. Love is the wish for others to be happy, for them to accomplish whatever their mind desires—whether it's material or mental— whatever they wish for in order to be fulfilled. This love and compassion is called *bodhichitta,* "awakened heart," because a mind that is enlightened naturally and unconditionally cares for the welfare of others. In Tibet bodhichitta is called *changchup sem.* We can take this to mean, "Until all beings achieve the level of a buddha, I will be courageous in working for the happiness of others." This expresses the motivation of the bodhisattva warrior, one who vows to develop his enlightened mind in order to help others.

What the Buddha discovered is that we all have bodhichitta, ripe for nourishment. Within the bewildering maelstrom of thoughts and emotions that keep our sense of self solid, each of us already has the seeds of love and compassion. Bodhichitta is the radiant heart that is constantly and naturally, without self-consciousness, generating love and compassion for the benefit of others. It's a stream of love and compassion that connects us all, without fixation or attachment. It has a tender sadness to it, like a wound that remains eternally exposed. It's our true nature. Cultivating this quality will soften our future because, given the proper conditions, the enlightened mind will blossom like a flower. When this happens, we will be in sync with how things really are.

The mind of enlightenment emerges whenever we find ourselves wishing for someone else's happiness without wanting anything in return. Bodhichitta is as big as that selfless moment when a parent would do anything to free a child of suffering. However, it can also be expressed in little ways, such as wishing that someone could have some food to eat or do well in their exam or work. That moment of delight and care is bodhichitta. It is our inherent awakeness peeking out like a jewel spontaneously arising from our open heart. It's our true wealth, a blessing that is always available. It can arise anywhere—in the middle of an argument, in the middle of reading a book, in the middle of a walk—whenever we feel the wish to help a child, an animal, an old person, a friend—unconditionally, with no expectations. It also arises in the feeling of compassion, when we want the pain of others—the cut on their finger, the cancer they suffer—to stop.

Throughout our lives we've experienced bodhichitta, but in a fleeting way. Sometimes we feel vast unconditional compassion or love—but then it fades, like the sun coming and going, or a shooting star. It is very vibrant, but it dissipates quickly. It feels like an anomaly because we're not used to it. It might have popped its head out, but we squashed it back. We didn't have space for this tender, open, courageous warrior heart to grow, because there was only room for "me"—my concerns, my wishes. Now that our minds are softer, more pliable, the natural joy of our being can expand. In contemplating bodhichitta, we're trying to mold our mind to the point where extending uncondi-tional love and compassion is our mainstay, our basic motivation.

To develop bodhichitta involves a fundamental change of attitude. The point is to gradually change the object of our meditation from ourselves to others. Our mind has been so used to facing inward that it will take a transformation for it to face outward. In fact, our whole existence has been turned inward, so it is going to take some massaging to turn it around. This shift is sparked by seeing that the habit of always thinking of ourselves only keeps us unhappy. To extend ourselves to others is the route to true happiness.

The point of this practice is that by feeling the love and compassion we have, we can make it bigger, with the aspiration that eventually, just like the Buddha, we will be able to extend our open hearts toward everyone we meet. To do that, we need to practice rousing bodhi-chitta regularly.

As with all contemplations, rousing bodhichitta depends on a strong and stable mind. With peaceful abiding as our base, we can bring a feeling to our hearts and keep it there without distraction. In turn, as we contemplate compassion and love, we are strengthen-ing our mindfulness. First we feel the love or compas-sion we have now for someone close to us. We saturate ourselves in this feeling and then gradually expand our circle to include acquaintances, "neutral" people, irritating people, and eventually all sentient beings. With cultivation, this mind of bodhichitta will arise spontaneously with whomever we encounter.

We begin our contemplation by resting in the open field of equanimity. With this attitude, we're letting go of fixed ideas of enemy and friend, which is our usual way of dividing up the world. We tend to have very strong opinions about who we love and who we don't, usually based on whether someone makes us feel good or bad. These concepts are changing all the time: a lover becomes an enemy, an enemy becomes a friend. The good guys become the bad guys and vice versa. We maintain this view in subtle ways: even among animals, for instance, we think of sharks as bad and bunny rabbits as good, butterflies as beautiful and mosquitoes as obnoxious. Now we're going to let go of our opinions and level the playing field. We want to develop unconditional love and compassion for everyone and everything. If we focus only on those we love, rousing bodhichitta will become an exercise in attachment.

When the Chinese invaded Tibet in 1959, everyone who could escape became a refugee. This included the Dalai Lama, other government and religious leaders, wealthy landowners, and the poorest nomads and farmers. When the refugees arrived in India, no matter what their social status had been in Tibet, none of them had a home. Everyone was equal. Ruler and subject, lama and monk, rich and poor alike had to make the best of being a political refugee in a foreign country. The field was leveled.

To encourage equanimity, we can take the attitude that everyone we encounter, directly or indirectly, has been kind to us. The driver of the bus takes us where we need to go. People work at night so we can read the news at breakfast. A total stranger grew the potato we ate at lunch. Even someone who irritates us might give us the time of day if we ask. If we believe in reincarnation, a traditional way in which we can elicit the attitude of equanimity is to imagine that at some point over many lifetimes every single sentient being has been our mother. Every single being we encounter has offered us the unconditional love and protection of a mother, as we have offered it to every single being. The person sitting next to us on the airplane has in one lifetime or another been our mother or father, friend or child or sibling. The point of invoking equanimity is to release our attachment to opinions, to let go of our relative notions of like and dislike.

With this attitude, we start where we are. We bring to mind someone for whom we feel tenderness, love, and care at this very moment. It could be our mother, our husband or wife, our child, a friend, or our cat or dog. The important thing is that when we think about this person or animal, our heart automatically goes out to them. One reason we feel love or compassion for this person is that they themselves care for us. We think of that person and our heart automatically gets bigger. Somehow they've brought joy, friendship, comfort to our life. When we think of their kindness, we wish to repay it. Our hearts are already open and connected. With no strings attached, we want them to be happy. We don't want them to suffer. So we begin our aspiration with what we wish for that person: "I hope that my brother has a safe journey," "May Diane's surgery be a success," or simply, "May David enjoy happiness." We connect with the love and compassion that we easily feel.

Accessing this immediate feeling makes a little crack in the hard ground around our heart. A beam of light comes out, like the tender shoots of a crocus poking through the ground in early spring. This is bodhichitta. We settle in that light, that growth; we rest there. We soften around it, we revel in it like a flower in sunshine. It feels refreshing and wonderful, and we only want it to grow bigger. More light comes through, more love, more care. We completely absorb ourselves in the natural joy of this bodhichitta. There's a sense of relief. It's like discovering that everything we ever wanted for others and ourselves is already contained in our own hearts. It's like waking from a dream. The longer we relax in this energy the bigger it gets.

Contemplating bodhichitta takes a lot of letting go. When we do this practice, what might come up are hopes and fears about our loved ones, negative thoughts about people whom we don't like or about painful events. We don't deal with these distractions by overriding them with the pretense of love. As we return to the words "May this one know happiness" or "May this one be free of suffering," something deeper than the emotional disturbance tells us that it's okay, we can let the anger dissipate. That something is bodhichitta expanding. Like the peace we experience in shamatha, this bodhichitta is intrinsic, a natural resting place. However, we must practice becoming familiar with it and train in making it bigger.

As we stabilize ourselves in the warmth and openness of our feeling for our loved one, we become able to radiate it in a wider arc. Now we make it big enough to include someone with whom we're not quite so close. We can start by wishing for the happiness of a neighbor or an acquaintance. "May Jared's friend get the job he wants." We begin to realize that just like our loved one, this person too deserves our care and kindness. If we feel more daring, we can wish people the root of happiness, which is that they discover their basic goodness. We can wish that they find their way out of bewilderment and suffering. Everyone deserves to be happy; no one deserves to suffer. Thus we extend this feeling to them. We're beginning to see that we have plenty of love and compassion to share. As we generate these feelings, they bring an actual sense of relief. It's like the sun melting a piece of ice in our heart into a warm inviting pool in which we can bathe. The more we do the practice, the bigger the pool gets, and the more people we can invite in to share it. This wealth is self-sustaining: the more we generate, the more we have.

Now we can extend our hearts to people we hardly know — on the street, at the office. We can look in their eyes and see in them that they're just like me, just like my child, just like my mother, my brother, my wife, my husband. We can even extend love and compassion to people we see on television, to people we read about in the newspaper. They may not be my wife or friend, but we all need love, we all need care. It's as if we are on fire with love and care for others. The happiness of others becomes our happiness. It's like inviting someone over for dinner. We make the food, and we're completely engrossed in whether they like it and if they're having a good time. If they're happy, it makes us happy.

Now the tender young shoot has grown into an enormous stalk. In generating love and compassion, we've entered the heart of the Buddha, where there is limitless love and compassion for all. It's a free-flowing energy that isn't even particularly ours, and it connects us with everyone, beyond the limitations of personalities and concepts. Now we can bring to mind people whom we don't even like and radiate the warmth of love or compassion to them.

Next we can extend bodhichitta to all sentient beings. We can use the aspiration "May all sentient beings experience happiness" or "May all sentient beings be free from suffering," and rest there in the middle of an enormous circle of fire that is burning so brightly that we no longer feel separate from any of them. This is the power of bodhichitta, the great mind of enlightenment. It is the mind of the bodhisattva warrior, who can care for all beings infinitely.

When we get up from our meditation session, we can keep the fire in our heart burning. We can carry that warmth, that intention to care for the well-being of others, into every moment of our lives. When we do that we are more awake to our enlightened qualities immediately. We're riding on windhorse—the energy of basic goodness that has been ours from beginningless time. If we are diligent in generating love and compassion, at some point it will spontaneously arise in any situation. It's like jumping into the heart of enlightenment, which is the same as our own heart. When we

awaken the heart of enlightenment, it's not simply what
we have, it is what we *are*.

If we spend part of the morning and part of the
evening generating bodhichitta, we can reflect back on
our day and feel genuinely good that we did something
worthwhile. We were courageous enough to take time
out from the "me" schedule to think of others. In order
for our mind to do that, it has to come out of itself. It
has to be less preoccupied with its own concerns. It has
to stretch just a little bit. In doing this, we're actually
extending love and compassion to ourselves as well.

It's not that we have to think about every single
other person on the planet all the time. Rousing bodhichitta means that we're actively engaging in thoughts
of both self *and* other, in subject *and* object. Just by
thinking beyond "me," we're recycling; we're giving
something back to the earth and to the world. Just by
thinking, "May *she* be happy," rather than "May *I* be
happy," we've begun to change the structure of our life,
and, to a certain degree, the structure of the whole
world. There are so many people on Earth—how many
of us are sitting on a cushion with a calm mind, generating love and compassion in our being? How many of
us even know that we can do this? Even if we know,
how many of us make time to do it?

When we generate this mind of enlightenment, we
discover that it produces happiness and peace in our-

selves. Contemplating, thinking about, and generating bodhichitta is a sure way to be happy, to be at peace. Having kindness and compassion in the face of suffering leads to the genuine desire to achieve enlightenment. That's why happiness is known as virtue in the Shambhala Buddhist tradition, because what virtue produces is more virtue. And how we experience virtue is happiness.

Four

WARRIOR IN
THE WORLD

Nineteen

Rousing Motivation

The Tibetan word for motivation is *künlong*. It means "to rise above, to come up." Rousing our motivation by making it bigger is how we rise above samsara. It takes courage to make our motivation bigger. The first step in expanding our motivation is to stop and notice what we're doing. We can start by asking, "What's the point of my life, its genuine meaning? What is my motivation in living this life?" The more we contemplate motivation, the more potent and powerful a force it becomes.

Traditionally there are a few different levels of motivation by which we might live. These motivations are the natural development of our human potential. The first motivation is to take care of our material needs. This is a commonsense motivation. We need to eat, dress, and stay warm. It's good to take care of our family and ourselves. If this is our only motivation, however, we're not fulfilling our human potential.

The second motivation is slightly broader: we combine our worldly aims with spiritual practice. Many practitioners in our culture are motivated by worldly concerns and use spirituality to successfully accomplish their wishes. It's fine to use spiritual practice to get what we want. People have always made offerings to the gods in order to ensure a plentiful harvest. It should be clear, however, that at the heart of this motivation lies the desire to please ourselves. The danger of this motivation is that we can trick ourselves into thinking that we're becoming less worldly when what we're really doing is distorting practice to fortify our comfort zone. This is a common pitfall, not a crime.

My father often taught about "cutting through spiritual materialism." This means cutting through our attempts to use spirituality to feed our solid self. The Buddha also taught that stability, the peace that comes through meditation, can become just as much a trap as any old desire. We can create a Goldilocks zone out of our practice and hide there. We can become "spiritual junkies," motivated only by what makes us feel good. So much of what passes as spirituality these days is really about pleasure seeking, getting high. This self-absorption disguised as spirituality only leads to more suffering. Real spirituality is about getting grounded. Once we understand who we are, we can realize the needs of others and do something about helping them. Being grounded in who we are is known as basic goodness.

Our motivation stretches further when we begin to think about how our current actions might affect us after death. This larger motivation comes from seeing the vast interconnection of cause and effect and the fact that our present activities directly affect what will happen to us in the future. With this motivation, we practice spiritual teachings to assure a favorable afterlife or rebirth, depending on our beliefs. In traditional Buddhist cultures, people are motivated by the desire to accumulate merit. Merit is like a series of domino chain reactions that enable positive results in this and future lifetimes. Tibetan nomads go on long religious pilgrimages, sometimes prostrating themselves for months on end across vast, desolate plains and mountain ranges. They do this to show their heartfelt devotion for the living teachings of the Buddha. But underneath their activity lies the motivation to do something now that will lead to larger future happiness.

Traveling in Tibet, I was so touched by the devotion of the nomadic people. Everyone makes offerings to the local monastery. People with almost no money give generously to teachers and monks. Whenever I was staying at a monastery, village people would line up for hours, pushing and shoving to be able to offer what little they had. People also spend their time carving mantras on stones and circumambulating sacred places. While meditating and making offerings is the foundation of their culture, their real motivation is to make things work out well for themselves later. They are less focused on "me" right now and more interested in how they can prepare for death as well as rebirth. They know that attaining personal enlightenment can take many lifetimes, so they're setting themselves up with meritorious activity in order to establish conditions for a favorable rebirth and ultimate enlightenment. In Buddhist terms this would mean being born human under circumstances in which we can hear and practice the dharma. This motivation is yet a larger version of the "have a nice day" approach. We're trying to get everything in order and make it work out in the long run. We want our nice day to last longer.

In the next, larger motivation we see clearly that the chain reaction of causes and conditions that dominate our world is cyclical, endless, and fundamentally dissatisfying. Perhaps we've struggled through one relationship after another, or we have continual problems with our family or at work. Something opens our eyes to the depth of bewilderment and the darkness of samsara. We see that pain, suffering, impermanence, and death are the facts of life.

When we enter into this larger motivation, we break out of thinking that we can get what we want from the circle of suffering. We see its endless quality, and we want the giant wheel to stop. Our motivation here is to break out of the cycle, and seek freedom from suffering.

All these motivations are considered small because they center on our own happiness, as opposed to the happiness of others. However, each one is slightly larger than the one before, because its perspective is bigger. What marks the border between small motivation and great motivation is a shift in focus from our own happiness to that of others. Using our lives to bring benefit to others is considered a great motivation. Having this motivation of the warrior bodhisattva is how we generate bodhichitta. Bodhichitta is the best mind we have, and rousing the courage to live from it is the greatest motivation there is. It's this motivation that leads to enlightenment.

Knowing *why* we suffer, knowing that there's something we can do about it, leads us to dedicate our life to the service of others, who suffer just as we do. Having already understood our own suffering, we are no longer fearful of it. We have the courage to extend genuine compassion to others, not because we think we're better than they are, but because we know we're all the same. We know that, just like us, they have basic goodness. We know that, just like us, they suffer because they don't know their own wealth. We know that just like us, they could awaken the mind of enlightenment by rousing bodhichitta. This gives birth to greater compassion. The more confident we become in our own natural state, the more we want to help others see theirs. This wisdom becomes the sun within our hearts and compassion becomes the moon that shines above.

This is the motivation of an enlightened being, the motivation that has no boundaries and extends as far as the mind itself. Bringing benefit to others could take many forms, but the ultimate benefit is to help others awaken from bewilderment and suffering by helping them see their basic goodness. We take the welfare of all beings to be our responsibility and strive for unsurpassed enlightenment as the means to bring about the same enlightenment in others. We're so intimate with the roots of bewilderment and suffering that we cannot help but feel love and compassion for everyone. We would go to the ends of the earth to alleviate the suffering of others. We would work for the benefit of others for thousands and thousands of endless lifetimes. Even though we may not believe that there are many lifetimes, our courage is that big. We have that kind of fortitude and visionary perspective.

This is the way of a warrior bodhisattva, a being inspired to attain enlightenment. Obviously it's a worthy motivation, but it's important to be honest with ourselves and to start where we are. We need the ground beneath our feet in order to walk farther. We can expand our motivation gradually. That's the point of becoming familiar with our motivation and beginning to rouse it. We do this by contemplating it.

Contemplating motivation requires the willingness to slow down, open up, and tune in to our life. What's going on right now? What's propelling us? Our motivation changes from day to day. Once we're aware that we *have* a motivation, we can always make it bigger, even when we're feeling stressed or overwhelmed. We can practice rousing it as a way to open our heart beyond our own suffering—to relax into the bodhichitta that connects us all.

In contemplating our motivation, we see that sometimes we're stuck in our hard, tightly closed mind. What will pull us out of our slump? Sometimes loosening up by taking a shower or a walk or a rest might be the way to open into a larger motivation. Perhaps we do some yoga or meditate for a few minutes in order to feel better, a little stronger. At some point we might see that getting comfortable cheers us up, but only for a little while. That's a glimpse of renunciation. Then our heart might soften a little as we think of our friend who was in a car accident and can't do yoga anymore. Compassion arises in our mindstream and we're no longer just thinking about our own well-being. Our heart and mind have softened and grown; just by caring for another, we have entered into the courageous motivation of awakened heart.

We each have the potential to ally our minds with this vast motivation. It requires knowing our own strength, which is why we meditate. We can soften and open ourselves beyond our tight circle in order to live life big. Taking this journey requires discipline, diligence, and fortitude, but like all journeys, it starts with one step.

Try it. Tomorrow morning when you open your eyes, sit up in bed, take a deep breath, and ask yourself: "Okay, what does my mind feel like? How am I going to approach this day? What's driving me?" Bring to mind some of the different motivations. Contemplate your motivation for a few seconds or as a five- or ten-minute ritual that begins your day. Every human being already has a motivation. You have an opportunity to get to know yours and to turn your mind to the motivation of the warrior bodhisattva.

The good news is that awakened heart is in harmony with the vast motivation. In fact, it *is* vast motivation. The mind of enlightenment is naturally big and open, caring and kind. It is only the discursiveness of our wild-horse mind and the baggage of our solid sense of self that keep us feeling small and claustrophobic. True happiness is opening the mind of enlightenment. How do we get from here to there? By rousing motivation. Our motivation is what paves the path from bewilderment and suffering to wisdom.

Twenty

Wisdom and
Emptiness

I spend a lot of time studying traditional texts on Buddhism. Studying is a deep exercise in understanding the teachings, and in a way it's like a strategy game that requires always being on the ball. I'll be reading along as some ancient master is describing his understanding of a topic like meditation. He is commenting on how to practice, what the mind should be like, what kind of motivation to have, and so forth. I'll be thinking, "This sounds really good!" Then at the end of the chapter I read, "By the way, this isn't the whole picture." And the text proceeds to describe in detail how all that was just said is only relatively true.

There is always farther to go on the spiritual path. We think that we've arrived at a place that is really "it," but then something pulls the rug out from under us, pushing us beyond that view into a deeper insight. It never quite works to build a comfort zone out of meditation. If we're meditating properly, our practice and understanding will always take us a little further than we might think we want to go. By resting in the true meaning of our contemplation, we're becoming familiar with our own wisdom. We're beginning to see reality as it is. Just as we open our perspective beyond what we ever thought it could be, our wisdom thrusts us into yet a vaster world. This is how we keep moving on the path. At each stage of contemplative meditation, we're encountering a deeper level of knowing.

The aspect of the mind that knows its own actions is *sheshin,* "awareness," "presently knowing." Our mind is always subject to being distracted by thoughts of what happened in the past and ideas of what could happen in the future, but the living experience is what is happening now. The mind comes in and out of existence on a momentary basis, and thus the ability to know also comes in and out of existence on a momentary basis. *Now* is a fleeting moment, but it is knowable. It's a moment of freshness, a full involvement in the immediate present. Meditation trains us in the awesome power of the mind to be completely present with what is happening *now.*

Awareness gives us the ability to know what we're doing, and insight — *vipashyana* — gives us the ability to penetrate it. We're no longer simply sauntering through or slipping by or spacing out, unaware of our own lives. The power of awareness tells us how the mind feels, what it's experiencing, the quality of our meditation, and how we're conducting it. It notices the transitory and illusory nature of thoughts, emotions, and concepts. Insight is the higher view that draws conclusions about what awareness sees. It penetrates phenomena, our mind, confusion—all that we encounter—and sees its true nature, its meaning. At this point, an amazing transformation takes place. The simple act of awareness combined with the reflective capacity of insight begins to develop a deeper element called *prajna*. Prajna is the mind's natural intelligence. The word means "best knowledge, highest knowledge, most sublime knowledge." It's the ability to know what *is*. In contemplating concepts like impermanence, the precious opportunity of being born human, and bodhichitta, we use conceptual understanding to open the doorway to our wisdom.

To understand the truth of reality, we have to have a mind that is not completely overwhelmed by prefabricated patterns and has roused the motivation to be truly compassionate in its quest. Our understanding is continuous and cumulative: we keep having little insights about the nature of reality, and they build upon each other. For example, the pain we feel when we hold on to our solid sense of self and the joy we feel when we rest in our natural state opens the door into compassion for the suffering of others.

Our relative wisdom—causal prajna—takes us beyond the concept of "me," directly into the reality of our experience. It creates the conditions for the final result, which is nonconceptual understanding.

What is nonconceptual understanding? It's the intuitive insight that knows the truth directly, not through reason or logic, but beyond the realm of thought. Let's say we've never seen the moon. Hearing about it paints a conceptual picture in our mind. Someone draws a moon in the sand for us and this makes it more concrete, but it's still only an idea. Then one clear night we see the moon reflected in water. Though this image seems closer to the truth, we still don't know the moon itself. Finally someone points to the sky and we see the moon directly. Now we know the moon. It's said that seeing is believing—yet nonconceptual understanding is beyond belief. The moon itself is beyond the words, the picture, the reflection, and the finger. This is where prajna takes us—beyond. True reality is without concept, beyond the duality of this and that. True prajna, true knowledge, is direct experience. It's knowing without the filter of self. Direct experience is wisdom itself—unborn, unceasing, neither still nor moving.

It's prajna that will take us beyond conceptual mind to discover basic goodness, step by step. It's prajna that will give us a glimpse into the totality of the heart of the universe, which is of the same nature as our own.

Through prajna we discover that there is no physical cohesion to what we see, yet appearances continue to arise. Our passion arises. What makes up the object of our desire? The very thing that hooks us—a feeling, a meal, or another person—is made of parts, and those parts can be broken down infinitely. When we look for a solid self, where is it? Is it in our feelings? Meditation has shown us how effervescent these are. Is it in our body? Then where? In the arms, the legs, the head, the heart? We can't find the self in any of these forms. Even if we come to the conclusion that we're all these parts, they don't hold together as a solid self. There's something more than form to us; there's also consciousness.

Consciousness comes in many forms. It also is not solid. There's a consciousness associated with sight, with sound, with taste, with touch, with smell. That's how we know what we perceive. We also have a mental consciousness, within which we have memories, ideas, and dreams. These memories, thoughts, and dreams are based on sense perceptions. These sense perceptions are how we know form. And with prajna we understand that those forms are not solid. One of the more provocative Buddhist teachings puts it this way: "Form is emptiness, emptiness also is form."

Our investigation begins to show us that "me," which at first seemed so solid, isn't solid at all. When we disassemble it, we can't find anything. Seeing the reality of no self is a preliminary understanding of profound emptiness. Yet all the same, we do perceive a self, and the world also appears to be quite real. Someone asked the Buddha about this: "If there's no self, who's this talking to you here, and what's this world I see?" He replied, "What you see are *skandhas*, heaps, aggregates. They are form, feeling, perception, mental formation, and consciousness." He placed rice on the ground and said, "The self is like this pile of rice. When you look at it, it seems to be one whole entity. When you look closer, it breaks down into grains of rice, and those grains of rice can be broken down still further. Thus things appear to have form, yet they are empty of form."

Contemplating the Buddha's words may just give us a small glimpse of emptiness, based on a conception. We may not believe what we see, but a seed of understanding is planted. This loosens up our solid sense of self. That's the beginning of prajna, the beginning of the mind being able to truly see what's happening. Prajna needs our involvement and our inquisitiveness. We may not experience ourselves as emptiness, but after contemplating it for a while, it's possible to come to the conclusion that yes, there is really no "me." This is how prajna begins to make sense of who we are—or are not—and of our environment as well. It is said that at the time of death this profound understanding dawns on us naturally because we feel our bodies falling apart, yet our consciousness remains and is able to know. All that was "me" has gone off in the ten directions. But if we contemplate the truth of emptiness now, we don't have to wait until that particular moment to discover it. Meditation is how we prepare ourselves for death—and for life. Meditation is a process of becoming comfortable with our own wisdom, which is direct experience of the ultimate truth.

For a very long time we've held the view that things exist and are real. When we begin to really look at things, when we start to break things down to a minute level, we see that there's nothing inherent. We can look as much as we want, but we'll never find anything that is solidly here. The ultimate truth is emptiness, suchness— in Sanskrit, *shunyata*. Emptiness is at the base of all that we experience. That's not to say that nothing exists on a relative level. Rather, there's an all-pervasive quality that something doesn't seem quite right, and that quality is emptiness. We mustn't be misled into thinking that emptiness is nihilism or nonexistence, because this emptiness transcends existence and nonexistence, both and neither. This is known as *ta shi trö trel,* "freedom from the four extremes."

This emptiness is inseparable from the wisdom inherent in our own mind. This emptiness of our wisdom mind has radiance. Thus the nature of wisdom mind is known as luminosity emptiness. In the same way, the sun shines inseparably from the empty space it inhabits. This suchness is the nature of all. It is basic goodness—simply what is. This is how an enlightened being experiences the world. Everything is inseparable luminosity and emptiness, whether we see it clearly or not. Prajna awakens the potential to see it directly, and this gives rise to great joy or bliss.

Prajna is where view and meditation meet. The view is our understanding, and practice is how we make it our own. If we want to understand the stability, clarity, and strength of our mind, we practice shamatha. If we want to begin to understand emptiness, we contemplate the self and try to find it. It isn't that we vault from taming the mind to contemplation into nonconceptual emptiness. We don't pledge our allegiance to the Buddha and prepare to jump. It's a gentle transition. Practicing shamatha has made our mind subtle and supple enough to understand these profound truths. The more we practice, the more we realize that the rock we're standing on—the fabricated self—is far from solid. Through practice and understanding, the rock begins dissolving. In discovering emptiness, we're not leaping anywhere. Practice wears away the rock, like water dripping for aeons. By the time we see what's happening, we've overcome our fear of falling off. We know the suffering caused by the simple misunderstanding that there was something to stand on. We *want* practice to wear away the illusion of a self.

Of course, keeping a grip on ourselves is an old and very deeply rooted pattern. It takes ongoing courage and hard labor to give it up. The fact of the matter is, however, that whether we hold on to it or give it up, the self has never existed. It's like a mirage. Within samsara we're never going to find true existence. Nor will we find it in nirvana. As long as we invest in this illusion, it's never going to be a perfect day; something's always going to go wrong. The pleasure we hope for is always turning into the pain we fear. Wisdom, on the other hand, is free from change.

Prajna is how we become familiar with the true nature of reality. We see that samsara is not a place, but a mistaken view, a way of freezing reality into a concept. We see how this pattern has led to our own suffering. We feel compassion because it's clear that everyone suffers from the same delusion, and it causes so much pain. This wisdom and compassion can lead to full enlightenment, full awakening from this dreamlike existence, complete knowledge and understanding of who and where we are (or are not).

Experiencing the true nature of reality brings great joy, *raptu gawa*. Directly seeing this suchness, we know that enlightenment is possible. We've climbed to the top of the hill and peeked over, and we see a beautiful lake and a meadow. We look back and see that others are struggling very hard up the hill. Like the Buddha, now we can say, "If it's possible for me, it's possible for everybody. I can go help bring those people up." This is the aspiration of the warrior bodhisattva and the basis of enlightened society.

Twenty-one

Warrior in the World

When we talk about enlightened society, we aren't talking about some utopia where everyone's enlightened. We're talking about a culture of human beings who know the awakened nature of basic goodness and invoke its energy in order to courageously extend themselves to others. Their motivation is allied with compassion, love, and wisdom. This enlightened attitude is not inhibited: it accommodates and incorporates the vicissitudes of life.

To meet our basic goodness, we meditate. Through peaceful abiding, we learn to rest fearlessly in our natural state. We see what an enlightened being sees: basic goodness is the ground of being, the nature of everything; it's an indestructible continuum, a diamond hologram with infinite facets. Through contemplation we discover that, like the reflection of a jewel in the sunlight, it is empty. In continuing to contemplate, we see that this emptiness is vibrant and dynamic—a playful display of thoughts, emotions, and perceptions. This is luminosity.

We experience basic goodness when we relax deeply into how things are, without wanting to change them. From that supple state, bodhichitta naturally flows. This is the mind of enlightenment. By using meditation to dissolve the illusion of "me," we ally ourselves with it. Now we can rely on its energy, just as we can rely on the energy of a horse. The majestic spirit of our wild-horse mind has been tamed and gathered into windhorse, the primordial energy of basic goodness. Our practice now lies in riding it.

We call it *windhorse* because its nature is uplifted, strong, exuberant, and brilliant. It's running and the mane is flying. When I was in Tibet I saw windhorse in the bearing of warriors on horseback who were dressed as King Gesar, Tibet's epic hero. Making the mind an ally gives us the power to ride the radiant windhorse in any situation. Riding the energy of basic goodness is like riding the rays of a sun that is always rising. In the Shambhala Buddhist tradition we call it the Great Eastern Sun. Everything we encounter shines with the dignity and splendor of basic goodness, and we see a sacred world. With this view, we are beginning to lay the foundation of an enlightened society.

How do we live from the stainless pure ground of basic goodness? How do we generate a compassionate heart in every encounter? How do we plant the flower of bodhichitta on the rock of a dark age? The quickest, most practical way to do this is to keep loosening our grip on ourselves. This is when windhorse is most accessible. It all comes back to one of my favorite sayings, "If you want to be miserable, think about yourself. If you want to be happy, think of others." This is how we bring enlightened mind down to earth.

When he achieved enlightenment, the Buddha used Earth as his witness. He later taught six *paramitas* — courageous ways to live on Earth. The word denotes a process: "arriving at the other side." We ground our behavior in these actions, which will keep us moving beyond small motivation into the sacred outlook of the Great Eastern Sun. Generosity, patience, exertion, discipline, meditation, and prajna are the enlightened activities of the warrior bodhisattva. It's the wisdom of prajna that makes them enlightened, transforming them from conventional virtues into ways to go beyond the darkness of samsara. Prajna uses the other paramitas to put bodhichitta into action.

The power of these activities is that they help us become comfortable with basic goodness. They support us in relaxing into the ground of our authentic being. They also support each other. Continuously offering in the spirit of generosity enriches the discipline of nonattachment. Discipline in keeping our heart and mind open increases patience. Having patience gives staying power to exertion. Acting with joyful exertion for the benefit of others strengthens meditation. The mind of meditation sharpens prajna, which sees things as they are. Prajna uses the other activities to keep activating bodhichitta, our lightest mind. It's light because it lacks the reference point of a self. This also gives us a sense of humor.

Generosity — *jinpa* — is the first paramita. It's the treasure of the warrior bodhisattva because it keeps us from holding on to ourselves. Because we have a pliable mind, we can let go. Generosity dispels self-centeredness and the desire to consume, which obscure basic goodness and dampen our ability to love.

Sometimes it's hard to be generous in our practice. Often when we try to generate love and compassion, we find that we can't extend our heart to those beyond our immediate circle. Even at the level of aspiration, we're stingy. We think, "Why would I care about those neutral people? What have they done for *me*?" We want so much for ourselves that we can't even offer the wish for others to be happy. We don't want to give — not even our thoughts and intentions. We wonder, "How can simply thinking help others?" But when we hear that someone's thinking about *us*, all of a sudden the table's turned and thoughts have great power.

In reality, what have we done for anybody? We keep taking and consuming, both psychologically and materially, and then we expect more. The beauty of rousing love and compassion is that it forces us beyond this small view. Visualizing someone else experiencing happiness in the face of our attachment strengthens our ability to let go. Our mind becomes lighter. It becomes very clear that our grudges and desires are habitual ways of holding on to ourselves. Rousing bodhichitta is a way to turn our attitude toward generosity. It propels us to start giving rather than taking.

Physical giving is a simple way to activate generosity. Giving clothing, gifts, money, time, or food liberates attachment and creates a conduit for love and compassion. At the moment we give, we are quite self-less. We can also offer words: giving condolences, comfort, confidence, courage, and strength. By generating an even larger intention as we're doing it—"May all beings benefit," "May I feed the whole world"—we're expanding our treasure.

I was amazed by the generosity of villagers in Tibet when I visited them in their very humble homes. They would offer me literally everything they had: pictures, rugs, pots, pans, yaks, sheep. Their uninhibited generosity was genuine. It wasn't as if they were hoping that I wouldn't take their offerings. If I accepted, they were incredibly happy. Yet sometimes in this world of plenty, we hide our box of chocolates when our friends come over. We're at the market looking at a beautiful display of fruit, and we want the person in front of us to get out of the way so we can have first pick.

Sometimes we're even stingy with ourselves. We buy an article of clothing and we can't let ourselves enjoy wearing it. We keep saving it for a special occasion. This level of greed only causes pain. Holding on to anything is a way of holding on to ourselves. The way to get to the other side is to give without hesitation. If we're simply too stingy to offer to others, we can start by giving something from our left hand to our right hand.

Once when I was with His Holiness Khyentse Rinpoche, a sick man came into the room, wanting a blessing to make him well. Rinpoche just held him like a father would. He didn't do anything special. He just let that person know he was okay. The most profound generosity we can offer is this kind of love and compassion. It doesn't matter whether somebody did something for us or not, we can offer our love and compassion. We can do it any time, anywhere. Even by meeting someone else's eyes, we let go of where we're holding back. The ultimate generosity takes place at the level of wisdom: knowing the giver, the recipient, and the gift to be pure and empty. This is the most profound generosity because there is no attachment.

The next transcendental activity is discipline, known as *tsültrim*. Discipline is the eyes of the warrior. It is closely allied with awareness. With discipline we hold our mind to the view of basic goodness, the stainless ground of being. We speak and act from bodhichitta—the genuine heart of tenderness that knows the richness and delight, the impermanence and suffering that dance upon that ground. Discipline is a long-term, wide-angle perspective that gives us the wisdom to live beyond deception and discursiveness.

Discipline sees the relationship between virtuous and nonvirtuous activities. In meditation we see that returning our mind to the breath or resting in the meaning of the words strengthens the mind of enlightenment. When we dwell in mental chatter, we become fearful and distracted. When we lose sight of love and compassion, we become stingy and angry. Discipline moves us beyond the ignorance of thinking we can do more or less what we want.

When we have the discipline to practice meditation consistently, our mind grows stronger. Within the container of discipline, we can relax. For example, one day my friend Jeff and I were golfing. He's a decent player, but on this particular day he'd somehow become very concerned about how far he could hit the ball. The more he tried to hit the ball, the worse his swing got. He was really playing very badly. I tried to talk to him about his swing, emphasizing that golf is about form, about elegance, as well as about how far the ball will go. By the time we got to the thirteenth hole, I said, "Your swing is so bad, for both our sakes I'm going to try to help you. If you'll let me, I'll give you a free ball." I worked with his stance, with his hands, with his posture. He said it felt strange. I told him to step up to the ball and do exactly what I said. He stepped up, took the swing, hit the ball, and said, "That felt really good." It was a beautiful shot. The ball flew about 175 yards, came back on the green, and went into the hole. Jeff said, "It works, it really works!" That's the power of discipline.

We use discipline to clear the road for the future by deciding what to do and not to do now. It's learning what to accept and what to reject. We're able to see more and more clearly the difference between virtue and nonvirtue—gewa and migewa. We see the nature of samsara and its pitfalls. Our minds are strong through practice, so we're not seduced into acting on negative emotions, even in our mind. We know such actions will create more pain for us. We turn our mind toward bodhichitta and wisdom instead. Through discipline we begin to understand how to maneuver in the realm of karma. Discipline looks at any situation and asks, "What is the action? What is the result?"

With discipline we gather virtuous qualities. Peacefully abiding is virtuous; radiating love and compassion is virtuous; understanding impermanence, emptiness, karma, and samsara is virtuous. Abiding by the six paramitas is virtuous. By living our life this way, we begin to see that harmonizing our view with our actions is how we continue to wake up. So we abandon what is negative and gather what is positive.

Discipline makes a container for enlightened activity. It sees when we're acting selfishly and when we're acting selflessly. It sees obstacles to our activity and applies the proper antidotes. For the warrior in the world, the most basic antidote to negativity is to radiate love and compassion.

Patience, *söpa*, is built on discipline. Patience is our saddle. Staying in the saddle doesn't necessarily mean waiting patiently for the doctor, the bus, or the airplane. For the bodhisattva warrior, patience is about overcoming anger and aggression. Aggression and anger are dangerous to the mind of enlightenment. In anger we become totally absorbed, enslaved, entrapped. Anger often leads to action. It gives us the urge to kill others, which denies them the opportunity to discover their enlightened minds. Even if we refrain from acting on it, anger has the power to annihilate our windhorse and destroy our love, compassion, wisdom, generosity, discipline, exertion, meditation, and prajna as well.

So we stay in the saddle of patience to counter that aggression.

By learning to hold our mind to an object in meditation, we train in patience. Then when a moment of anger arises in our everyday life, we might be able to hold our speech, hold our action. We don't jump out, lash out, or act out. If we're really dedicated to practicing patience, we even learn to generate love and compassion on the spot when anger arises. It's possible: in that moment we're about to become angry, with discipline we can see what's happening and turn our mind to enlightenment instead. Even if we do this only briefly, it strengthens our practice tremendously.

Patience means not resisting the nature of reality. We have the fortitude to stay in the saddle of big view and motivation. We don't mind wading through the river of impermanence. We enjoy riding across the plains of emptiness. We are happy even in difficult situations. We want to work for the welfare of others as long as it takes for everyone to realize the mind of enlightenment.

From patience comes exertion—*tsöndru*. Exertion is our indestructible armor. It gleams with joy. With exertion we celebrate basic goodness by extending our windhorse to others. We can do this because we've overcome laziness. We no longer dread practicing bodhichitta, because we know it's who we are. We practice exertion with the carefree delight of a dusty elephant who jumps into a pool of water on a hot day. There is no way that the elephant won't jump into that pool. This is how enthusiastic we feel in exerting ourselves for the benefit of others.

Rousing bodhichitta is an occasion for continual delight. We can hardly wait to raise it again. If we were the only person in the whole world to be generating love and compassion, we would generate it with fearless joy and delight until the day we die. Our aspiration to help others is so great that we would gladly spend an eternity in hell even to help a child be less afraid to speak in class.

Why are we so happy? Because we're free of "me." Working to make "me" happy only causes pain. Working for the happiness of others brings joy. We're not practicing bodhichitta because it's good for us; we're practicing it because we know the living empty brilliant truth of basic goodness. When we know this truth, extending love and compassion is all there is to do. We no longer swim against the current of reality. This is the basis of our conduct as warrior bodhisattvas. Radiating the warmth of love is pure simplicity; generating the cool rays of compassion is a relief; maintaining the illusion of a solid separate self is drudgery—hard labor with no sense of satisfaction. We no longer look for loopholes for how we can get out of practicing bodhichitta.

We must use common sense, however. It's important to attend to ourselves first. It's like putting on our own oxygen mask when the airplane loses altitude; then we can help others put on theirs. Also, we shouldn't take on projects that are too big, that we're unable to finish. For example, the people who travel with me when I go to India each year to study are often overwhelmed by the poverty and suffering they see. It makes them feel frantic—how will we help all these people? Too big an approach will only dishearten us, undermine our activity. Perhaps we start with just one person, one family. It's important to pick acts of compassion or kindness that we can complete. Then we can make the next one slightly bigger. It may not always be a smooth ride, but we never give up. We now see clearly that every action is an opportunity to ripen the mind of enlightenment, and we really want to go forward. The armor of exertion is also the armor of joy.

The next paramita is meditation, *samadhi,* which means "fully absorbed." By riding this horse we continue to let go of ourselves and renounce the path of selfishness. We are totally stable in our renunciation and continual abandonment of samsara. We are intimately familiar with the endless cycle of suffering that comes through thinking that the self is real and trying to gratify it. We're committed to looking at the many ways samsara aims to trap us. We never let ourselves forget that in samsara lies no happiness. We are completely committed to letting go of the view of "me." If we fall off the horse by acting selfishly, the paramita of meditation helps us regain our balance almost instantly. We're such experienced riders that we float with the horse's movement.

We are completely one-pointed in our allegiance to the path of the warrior. The mind of basic goodness is our ally. We use its strength and clarity to move out of the darkness of bewilderment and suffering with the open heart of bodhichitta. Bodhichitta envelops us like sunlight on a mountain. Generating love and compassion is our natural response to any situation. We know that moving forward in the wisdom of the Great Eastern Sun is the best way to renounce samsara.

This ability to renounce samsara leads to the next paramita, prajna, the highest form of knowing. Prajna is a double-edged sword that arises from our meditative experience. It gleams silver in the sun of basic goodness, mirroring the stainless purity of everything just as it is. The mind that knows the truth of reality is potent and powerful, like a laser beam. It alone can free us from the delusion that we exist. It cuts through the walls of bewilderment and ignorance and makes them obsolete. It burns through confusion, jealousy, anger, self-deception, hesitation, and doubt—any habitual pattern that wants to solidify our view, our meditation, or our activity. It sees what *is* and lights the way to liberate others from the bewilderment that keeps them trapped in the darkness of suffering. This sword is the ultimate weapon of the bodhisattva warrior.

Generosity, discipline, patience, exertion, meditation, and wisdom keep turning our mind to enlightenment like a flower seeking sunlight. This brings genuine delight. The more awake we are, the more connected we feel with other sentient beings. The more awake we are, the more we want to help others achieve the same freedom.

How do we help? How do we help others see their basic goodness, learn to touch their broken open hearts? How do we lead others to the mind of enlightenment? In describing the motivation of bodhichitta, the Buddha used the image of a shepherd herding his sheep in front of him. This may not be very practical: how could we encourage others into full enlightenment before we have gotten there ourselves? It might be more realistic to see ourselves as warrior kings and queens, riding our windhorse with majesty, elegance, and richness. We can take the paramitas as a code of enlightened behavior. We can use these qualities as currency in our transactions with others. This is how we can inspire others to discover their own basic goodness. This is how we can encourage them to follow the path of warriorhood. This is how we can help. Our intention is that of a shepherd, but our actions are those of a loving, wise, compassionate leader. If we all act according to this code, we will create an enlightened society.

We can take this image to heart in going about our daily activity. If we're driving on the freeway, if we're working in an office, if we're having dinner with our friends, if we're changing diapers, if we're at the movies, we can visualize ourselves sitting tall in the saddle of patience astride the horse of meditation. Our eyes are the eyes of discipline. Close to our heart rests the treasure of generosity. We are protected by the armor of exertion, and in our right hand we hold the gleaming sword of prajna. We are riding on the rays of the Great Eastern Sun, endlessly and courageously for the benefit of all.

With the mind as our ally and this code of enlightened behavior, it is our duty and joy to serve others. This doesn't mean becoming a doormat; it means seeing clearly what the skillful action is in every situation. That is living from the mind of enlightenment. Generating love and compassion is how we live our lives in full bloom. If we don't make progress in this way, we are strengthening the circle of suffering instead: doing the same self-serving things year after year, getting closer and closer to death. That's a waste of time, a waste of windhorse. When we live life in service to ourselves, our life force naturally diminishes.

How do we avoid wasting ourselves? By including meditation in our daily life and by rousing our enlightened qualities whenever we can. If we feel disheartened or depressed, visualizing a horse running through a beautiful meadow will stimulate a sense of empowerment. It gives us lightness and levity, as though anything is possible. This incredibly potent life force is windhorse. We always have the opportunity to raise it here and now. Saddling up and riding it is how we become the kings and queens of our own lives.

The journey of the bodhisattva warrior starts with the basic attitude of enlarging our motivation to include the welfare of others. This is a simple response to this dark age. Let's begin right now by engaging love and compassion however we can—not tomorrow, but today. By cultivating courage and confidence in ourselves and maintaining our seat, we can enjoy creating a sane environment; we can enjoy creating an enlightened society. This doesn't have to be overwhelming. Start by looking at your own life and see what you can do, one step at a time. Love is the saving grace. It's the buddha in you standing up and saying, "Even though it's dark, I have this jewel."

By this merit, may all obtain omniscience
May it defeat the enemy, wrongdoing
From the stormy waves of birth, old age, sickness, and death
From the ocean of samsara, may I free all beings.

By the confidence of the Golden Sun of the Great East
May the lotus garden of the Rigdens' wisdom bloom
May the dark ignorance of sentient beings be dispelled
May all beings enjoy profound, brilliant glory.

Appendix A

Preparing to Practice

The best support for regular and consistent meditation practice is that we enjoy doing it. If we prepare for it properly and make it a regular part of our life, it becomes like drinking water. So before we get to the cushion, we need to look at our lifestyle and prepare for practice properly.

The basic premise of meditation is "not too tight, not too loose." We can apply the principles of gentleness and precision in every aspect of the practice. Without precision we'll be unable to establish a strong container in which our practice can thrive. So we establish a routine, follow it with discipline, and stick to the instructions. Without gentleness, meditation will become just another way in which we're trying to measure up against a hopeless ideal. So we provide ourselves with the time and space to meditate, respect our limits, and soften up our minds and bodies properly. It's important not to expect perfection or get hooked on the finer points of the instruction. With gentleness and precision, meditation practice will bring us joy.

Beginning meditation practice is an excellent opportunity to contemplate how we spend our time. How much of what we do is important and truly necessary? One of the obstacles to meditation is being pulled in too many directions. What drains us; what nourishes us? Are there activities we can postpone or eliminate? It will be helpful to ask questions like these at the outset. Awareness lays the ground for a strong commitment to practice. Taming our mind isn't a hobby or an extracurricular activity—it's the most important thing we could be doing. It can even help streamline a pressured situation because it gives us clarity, peace, and fortitude. So while we may need to simplify our life in order to meditate, a benefit of meditation is that it will make our life simpler.

The next step is to establish a basic routine for meditation. When will you practice, and where? For many people, meditation works well in the morning, for others, evening is better. Some people find it effective to sandwich their day between two short sessions. Experiment with different times until you discover what's best. Once you settle on a regular time, stick to it. This is how to develop a daily rhythm of meditation. Establishing a definite practice time frees you of having to plan from day to day.

You can also free yourself from worrying about how long you will practice. If you decide to meditate for twenty minutes, stay on your seat for that period of time unless the house is on fire. Use a timer so that you can just relax into the practice without thinking about the minutes passing.

A successful meditation practice is a consistent practice. The best way to do shamatha or contemplation is in short sessions consistently for a very long time. Ten to twenty minutes of sitting practice a couple of times daily over a lifetime is good. Of course we can do longer sessions whenever we want. It's better to do consistent shorter sessions over a long period of time, however, than to do longer sessions sporadically or not at all. The recipe that works for most people is short sessions every day. Doing short sessions at the beginning and end of the day is very good for stabilizing the mind. If you're not able to meditate every day and you decide to do it twice or three times a week, the important thing is just to stay with it. Adapt your practice to your schedule. When you have less time, do shorter sessions.

If we meditate haphazardly, doing a big session of practice one day and not returning to the cushion for a month, we won't enjoy meditation. That approach is frenzied and stressful, like digging a big hole in the garden and then forgetting about it. When we return, we have to start from scratch. Meditation in spurts is uncomfortable and painful because it can't ride on the cumulative effect of regular practice. We have to keep starting over. We need to apply ourselves consistently. Sitting for short sessions on a regular basis is a more gentle approach. One of the most common reasons that people stop meditating is that they mismanage their time.

Being ambitious about having the perfect situation for practice can also work against us. I have a student who began with meditation practice in his twenties and was quite disciplined with a regular practice of an hour a day. Then as he became busy with his career, he couldn't keep the schedule going, and his practice dropped away. He told himself that once he got more stability in his life he would begin to sit again. But then he got married and had a family. Having a regular hour-long practice became an even more remote possibility. Instead of simply shortening his sessions and letting his life fall into place around practice, he got caught thinking that he could create a perfect lifestyle to accommodate his longer sessions. As a result, he didn't practice at all for a very long time.

One of the simple things that you can do is to create a proper environment for practice — a place that is comfortable, quiet, and clean. A corner of your room that feels uplifted, safe, spacious, and private is good enough. It's worth investing in a proper meditation cushion. If you find ritual appealing, set up a table with candles, a flower, incense, pictures—whatever inspires you—and meditate in front of that. But again, don't get caught up in chasing your idea of the perfect environment in which to meditate. Some people from the city will go into the mountains to meditate in peace and find that the crickets and the birds won't shut up.

When I was in my teens, I went on several practice and study intensives with Lama Ugyen Shenpen, one of my tutors. On our retreats he always insisted that we wash and dress properly in the morning, even though we stayed in rustic cabins in the mountains, miles from anyone to see. He was just passing on what he'd learned from being on retreat with great masters in Tibet, who taught the importance of taking good care of ourselves and our meditation environment. Having some sense of basic dignity in our appearance and environment helps support meditation practice.

In Tibet and other Buddhist countries, lamas, monks, and nuns wear robes. While we in the West might regard robes as the lowest common denominator of clothing, the Buddha taught his disciples to wear robes with dignity, even specifying that the robes be evenly hemmed and that they fit properly. He taught that dressing well—even in robes—is a way to respect the teachings as well as respecting others and ourselves. Again, it's a matter of dignity: we're presenting ourselves to others so that we are pleasant to look at, and we're respecting our body and our practice that way.

This kind of uplifted attitude extends to working with our bodies and nourishing ourselves. We're all aware of how our mind influences what we can do with our body. Conversely we don't always consider how much influence our body has on our mind. If our body is hungry or in pain, it's hard to stabilize our mind. They have to be in harmony. Openness and flexibility of body encourages those same qualities in the mind. A supple body helps support our sitting meditation.

Yoga is a traditional and powerful way to open up the body's energy as well as develop flexibility. When I'm on retreat in India, I have the privilege of studying with one of the greatest living masters, Pattabhi Jois. He's taught me the benefits of doing yoga postures beforehand as one of the most effective ways to relax into meditation practice. I try to take the time to stretch before sitting down. Of course, while yoga is relaxing and energizing, it isn't a substitute for formal meditation. They are two different practices. Even in the ancient Hindu systems, the purpose for holding the various postures has always been to prepare the student to work with the mind and develop wisdom.

Practicing a martial art, doing tai chi or chi-gung, or simply getting regular exercise are all good ways to prepare the body for meditation. Of course, the traditional disciplines that work with inner energies and consciousness will have more in common with shamatha and contemplation. For this reason, we have our own system of yoga and Tibetan body-training in the Shambhala community. Eating properly is another way to support our practice.

Whatever happens in meditation arises from daily life. If we've had a hectic day, for instance, we have to put that into the equation. When I was training horses, I couldn't just barge into the stable, drag the horse out, throw it on the lunge line, and start trying to train it. I had to be sensitive to how the horse was feeling that day. Did it look a little heavier? Was the head down, were the ears back? What was the tail doing? Was the horse trying to smell me or was it backing off? In the same way, we need to realize that in terms of our practice, today is always going to be slightly different from yesterday.

Preparing the mind begins with stopping for a moment to see what our mind feels like. This is like stepping back and examining the horse we're about to ride. Since the way we feel changes all the time, our practice will need to change as well. Be compassionate and honest about your own needs and, at the same time, apply the necessary discipline. For example, if you're feeling agitated, it might be a good idea to take a slow walk outside before beginning your session. If you're drowsy, you might take a cool shower to wake up before you sit. Perhaps you'd like to read a little about meditation to remind yourself why you are practicing.

We also need to be sensitive to what we're thinking as we come into our session. If we just plop down on our cushion straight from the office or right after an argument, the entire meditation period might be spent slowing our mind down enough even to remember that we're meditating. We learn to leave certain things behind. It's like getting into bed. If you sleep naked, you take off all your clothes first. If you leave your jacket and shoes on, you'll be uncomfortable. In meditation we let go of as much as we can before we sit down. Most days we'll have enough discursiveness to handle just under ordinary circumstances.

Here's a helpful exercise for physical "checking in" before you sit. Stand with your arms relaxed at your sides, eyes either half-closed or shut. Slowly guide your attention up from your feet to the crown of your head. Pause where you find tension or imbalance, and breathe into those areas, allowing the tension to dissolve. Be aware of your body in the space; feel the support of the ground beneath your feet. Breathe deeply through your nose, exhaling stress, agitation, and tension. Be aware of your body. This exercise allows us to tune in and relax instead of rushing into meditation.

The essence of all of this preparation is really simple: when we sit down to meditate, we're eliminating all other activities. We choose the time and space wisely to reduce distractions. We prepare our body to relax before we sit. We prepare our mind to be as simple and present as we can be. And we do all of this with precision, as well as gentleness. But remember, this is just preparation, not actual meditation. If you try to create ideal conditions, you may never get to the cushion. At some point you just have to sit down and do it.

Appendix B

The Posture of
Meditation

1. The spine is upright, with a natural curve.
2. The hands are resting on the thighs.
3. The arms and shoulders are relaxed.
4. The chin is slightly tucked.
5. The eyelids are half shut.
6. The face and jaw are natural and relaxed.
7. If you're sitting on a cushion, keep your ankles loosely crossed. If you're sitting on a chair, keep both feet firmly on the floor.

Appendix C

Instructions for Contemplative Meditation

1. Calm the mind by resting on the breathing.
2. When you feel ready, bring up a certain thought or intention in the form of words.
3. Use these words as the object of meditation, continually returning to them as distractions arise.
4. In order to help rouse the heartfelt experience of their meaning, think about the words. Bring ideas and images to mind to inspire the meaning.
5. As the meaning of the words begins to penetrate, let the words drop away, and rest in that.
6. Become familiar with that meaning as it penetrates.

7. Conclude your session and arise from your meditation with the meaning in your heart. "Meaning" is direct experience, free of words.

8. Now enter the world aspiring to conduct yourself with the view of your contemplation. For example, if you have been contemplating the preciousness of human birth, your view will be one of appreciation.

Resources

For information regarding meditation instruction or inquiries about a practice center near you, please contact one of the following:

Shambhala International
1084 Tower Road
Halifax, NS
Canada B3H 2Y5
phone: (902) 425-4275, ext. 10
fax: (902) 423-2750
website: www.shambhala.org. This website contains information about the more than 100 centers affiliated with Shambhala.

Shambhala Europe
Annostrasse 27
50678 Cologne
Germany
phone: 49 (0) 700 108 000 00
website: www.shambhala-europe.org
e-mail: europe@shambhala.org

Karmê Chöling
369 Patneaude Lane
Barnet, VT 05821
phone: (802) 633-2384
fax: (802) 633-3012
e-mail: karmecholing@shambhala.org

Shambhala Mountain Center
4921 Country Road 68C
Red Feather Lakes, CO 80545
phone: (970) 881-2184
fax: (970) 881-2909
e-mail: info@shambhalamountain.org

Dechen Chöling
Mas Marvent
87700 St. Yrieix sous Aixe
France

phone: 33 (0) 5-55-03-55-52
fax: 33 (0) 5-55-03-91-74
e-mail: dechen-choling@shambhala.org

Dorje Denma Ling
2280 Balmoral Road
Tatamagouche, NS
Canada B0K 1V0
phone: (902) 657-9085
e-mail: denma@shambhala.org

Gampo Abbey
Pleasant Bay, NS
Canada B0E 2P0
phone: (902) 224-2752
e-mail: gampo@shambhala.org

Meditation cushions and other supplies are available through:

Samadhi Cushions
30 Church Street
Barnet, VT 05821
phone: (800) 331-7751
website: www.samadhistore.com
e-mail: info@samadhicushions.com

Naropa University is the only accredited, Buddhist-inspired university in North America. For more information, contact:

Naropa University
2130 Arapahoe Avenue
Boulder, CO 80302
phone: (800) 772-6951
website: www.naropa.edu

Information about Sakyong Mipham Rinpoche, including his teaching schedule and a gallery of photographs, is available at his website:

www.mipham.com

Audio- and videotape recordings of talks and seminars by Sakyong Mipham Rinpoche are available from:

Kalapa Recordings
1678 Barrington Street, 2nd floor
Halifax, NS
Canada B3J 2A2
phone: (902) 421-1550
fax: (902) 423-2750
website: www.shambhalashop.com
e-mail: shop@shambhala.org

The *Shambhala Sun* is a bimonthly Buddhist magazine founded by the late Chögyam Trungpa Rinpoche and now directed by Sakyong Mipham Rinpoche. For a subscription or sample copy, contact:

Shambhala Sun
P.O. Box 3377
Champlain, NY 12919-9871
phone: (877) 786-1950
website: www.shambhalasun.com

Buddhadharma: The Practitioner's Quarterly is an in-depth, practice-oriented journal offering teachings from all Buddhist traditions. For a subscription or sample copy, contact:

Buddhadharma
P.O. Box 3377
Champlain, NY 12919-9871
phone: (877) 786-1950
website: www.thebuddhadharma.com

ABOUT THE AUTHOR

Born in India in 1962, Sakyong Mipham Rinpoche is the spiritual and family successor of his father, Vidyadhara the Venerable Chögyam Trungpa Rinpoche. He is the living holder of the Shambhala Buddhist tradition, a lineage that descends through his father's family, the Mukpo clan. This tradition emphasizes the basic goodness of all beings and teaches the art of courageous warriorship based on wisdom and compassion. The Sakyong is an incarnation of Mipham Jamyang Gyatso (1846–1912), one of the most revered meditation masters and scholars of Tibet. Educated in Buddhist meditation, philosophy, and ritual, Sakyong Mipham Rinpoche was raised in both Eastern and Western traditions. Each year he retreats to India for study and practice. He also teaches at Shambhala centers throughout the world.

For more information see Sakyong Mipham's website at www.mipham.com.